LITTLE PINE TO KING SPRUCE

A Franco-American Childhood

LITTLE PINE TO KING SPRUCE

A Franco-American Childhood

Fran Pelletier

Tilbury House Publishers
Gardiner, Maine

TILBURY HOUSE, PUBLISHERS
2 Mechanic Street
Gardiner, ME 04345
800–582–1899
www.tilburyhouse.com

First edition October 2003 • 10 9 8 7 6 5 4 3 2 1

Library of Congress Cataloging-in-Publication Data
Pelletier, Fran, 1925-
  Little pine to king spruce : a Franco-American childhood / Fran
Pelletier.— 1st ed.
    p. cm.
  ISBN 0-88448-254-5 (pbk. : alk. paper)
  1. Pelletier, Fran, 1925—-Childhood and youth. 2. Children—
Maine—Diaries. 3. French-Canadians—Maine—Diaries. 4.
Canadians—Maine—Diaries. 5. Canadian Americans—Maine—
Diaries. 6. Maine—Social life and customs. 7. Maine—Biography.
I. Title.
CT275.P55225 A3 2003
974.1'004114'0092—dc22

                                                    2003017448

Cover designed on Crummett Mountain by Edith Allard,
        Somerville, Maine.
Editing and production by Jennifer Bunting and Barbara Diamond.
Layout by Tilbury House.
Printing and binding by Maple Vail, Kirkwood, New York.
Covers printed by the John P. Pow Company, South Boston.

DEDICATION

I would like to dedicate this book to my dear friends from the Washington Depot, Connecticut, Senior Writers' Group, and to Jean Sands, in particular, whose faith in my writing talents were far greater than my own. My nearly six-year association with the members of that group were among the happiest years of my life. We shared so many memories together while we bolstered each other's efforts, forming friendships that will ever endure.

It was Jean, our mentor, our teacher, and the moderator of our group to whom I am most indebted. A talented free-lance writer herself, Jean gave unsparingly of her time, her knowledge, and her experience as a writer to guide and help us fulfill our dreams and writing aspirations. Her greatest achievement was not in teaching us how to craft a story, essay, or poem, but in convincing us that we really could write well enough so that others would want to read our work. Without her encouragement, I would have given up long ago. I wrote for her as much as for myself. Her comments and her delight in whatever I produced were an inspiration to write yet another piece, which I hoped would be even better.

I am delighted to have produced a collection of stories deemed worthy of publication by Tilbury House, but without Jean's encouragement and stimulus I would still be a wannabe writer, always writing, always thinking about writing, and always unpublished. Thank you, Jean, for being the "genie" in my word processor that gave life and substance to my cherished memories.

Fran Pelletier
New Harbor, Maine

Table of Contents

	Preface	viii
1.	Pinettes, Spruces, and Pelletiers	1
2.	Summers with Grampy	9
3.	First Communion	15
4.	A Capital Trip	22
5.	The Lindbergh Suit	33
6.	The Big Snowstorm	42
7.	Taking Grampy Back	49
8.	Pig Tales	63
9.	The Derailment	83
10.	Cranberrying	93
11.	The Perfect Trees	99
12.	A Suit for Lawrence	108
13.	The Air Circus	118
14.	Puppy Love	131
15.	The Difference Between 'Em	142
16.	Evils of the Weed	152
17.	No Place to Spit	164
18.	That's Not the Road	171
19.	Fergus's Farting Horses	180
20.	The Trout	188

PREFACE

This book came about when my wife and children asked me to write down the many stories I had told them of my childhood in Milford, Maine—stories about my extended family and the many neighbors and acquaintances who made these stories what they are. I loved all of these individuals dearly and write of them fondly, recalling their humanity and their frailties with equal respect.

All these stories are based on actual events, but I have taken the liberty of combining some, enlarging others, and changing some names to make them stories, rather than mere facts. I hope my readers will enjoy them and be generous in their criticism if they remember some of the details differently.

To set the scene and add a little clarity to a family tree that has two grandfathers named Joseph, two uncles named Raymond, and even two cousins named Raymond:

My mother, Frances Mary Spruce, was the second-youngest of the seven children of Joseph and Helen Spruce. My father was the second oldest of the seven children of Joseph and Dorilda Pelletier. Joseph Spruce was a merchant and postmaster in Milford. His store had various names at different times but was commonly called Spruce's Store. It became R. J. Spruce and Son sometime in the 1920s when my grandfather sold it to his son and daughter-in-law, Raymond and Essie Spruce.

My Uncle Ray continued to employ as many of his family as possible in the store. My father—his brother-in-law—was the butcher and general clerk for many years, so the store figures as an important place in my childhood. My Grampy Spruce continued on in the store and kept the post office there until the 1940s, when he retired and his youngest son, Wilfrid, became postmaster in his stead.

My Pelletier grandparents lived on South Main Street in Old Town, Maine, just across a bridge from Milford. Grampy Pelletier worked parttime for the Maine Central Railroad as a flag station attendant in his later years. He also owned woodlots from which he cut firewood and pulpwood to sell. He had once been a woodsman in the North Woods, where he started as a woodcutter but later became a cruiser and scaler.

Each of my parents had a brother named Raymond. Mama's brother had a son named Raymond, and we differentiated between the two by calling the father Ray and the son Raymond. On Dad's side, it was more complicated in that while his brother Ray was unmarried, their sister Edna had a boy whom she named Raymond. Since they all lived with my grandparents, we called Edna's son "Little Ray."

The Pelletiers and the Spruces all got along well, and there were times when both families took pleasure in outings together. I hope you enjoy meeting them, along with our friends and neighbors. I certainly enjoyed them in real life.

Fran Pelletier
New Harbor, Maine

1

PINETTES, SPRUCES, AND PELLETIERS

I was born on November 23, 1925, in Old Town, Maine. My parents were Frances Mary Spruce and Emile Joseph Pelletier. Both were of French-Canadian heritage—my father more so than my mother. My paternal grandparents were both French-speaking and had a long French-Canadian lineage.

My mother's father was of French-Canadian ancestry, although his family name of Spruce led many to think he was of English ancestry. The family name had been Pinette or Pinet until my great-grandfather, Jeremy, and his brothers decided to Anglicize the family name about the time of the Civil War.

According to my grandfather, the name was changed because the brothers Pinette recognized that there was some discrimination and prejudice against people of French-Canadian background in the town of Bradley, Maine, where they lived. They had come from French Canada in 1850 to find work in the lumber industry that was the mainstay of the Maine economy at the time. The forests of Maine were supplying much of the lumber for the country and to some extent for Europe. Spruce, of which there was an abundance in Maine, was the lumber of choice. It was strong, light, and the trees grew long trunks, making for knot-free boards. All other trees were thought to be inferior for house-building. Spruce was king.

Translated literally, Pinette means "little pine." The Pinette brothers could have changed their name to "Pine," but they knew that the abundant pine in Maine was thought to be suitable only for ship's masts; the virgin pines were huge and made great masts for the wooden ships of the era. Their wood was sold by the ton, and it was called "ton lumber."

But its general low esteem made Pine a poor choice for a family name. It indicated something second-rate, a junk tree. Who would want to be known as a Pine? But spruce! Ah, that was different. That tree was commonly referred to as "King Spruce." Spruce was a name worthy of the Pinette brothers, so Spruce it was, and Spruce it stayed.

My grandfather Joseph Spruce moved to Milford in 1870 where he worked in a general store for ten years before marrying Helen Caroline Dudley, the daughter of a Yankee lumber mill foreman and Congregationalist. The Dudleys were the Cabots of Milford. They spoke only to God and took a dim view of their only daughter eloping (to Waterville) with a French-Canadian—and a Catholic, to boot! But the marriage was strong from the start, and the newlyweds were able to overcome family disapproval on both sides. In partnership with an older brother, Joe ended up buying the store from Marshall Sawyer, Esq., and in 1900 was appointed postmaster. My own father ended up working at the store after he married my mother. By then it was called R. J. Spruce & Son.

Joe and Helen Spruce had seven children together. My mother, Frances Mary, was the youngest girl and the second-youngest child. She grew up Catholic, for Helen converted to Catholicism so strongly that she almost made the Pope look like a Baptist.

My mother grew up in Milford and never learned to speak French. She was more Yankee than French-Canadian despite being educated in the French-speaking convent school, but when she married my father she married into a French-speaking family that was close-knit and still kept most of the ethnic traditions of French Canada.

Dorilda Langlais Pelletier, my paternal grandmother, was a strong-willed, intelligent woman who had been educated in a private Catholic girls' school in Lewiston, Maine. She was not thought to be a great beauty, but was spoken of as handsome, which in those days meant she was plain. She married Joseph Damase Pelletier, an illiterate young woodsman who was very handsome and very ambitious. Her parents thought she married beneath herself, but her marriage flourished.

My Grandfather Pelletier had been born in French Canada, in the Gaspé Peninsula town of St. Alexander de Pocatiere, and had come to Old Town in 1871 at the age of six with his parents. Grampy told me many times of how he had lived in what was called "the French settlement" of West Old Town, where the family lived on a small farm near Pushaw Stream. I vaguely remember going there once with Dad and Grampy when I was very small to visit with Grand-mamère, who lived in a tiny house with dirt floors. Grand-mamère was a wispy, shriveled woman with iron-gray hair, who sat rocking incessantly while clouds of tobacco smoke wreathed her head like a halo as she smoked Edgeworth tobacco in an old and smelly corncob pipe. Grand-mamère was very old and wrinkled, and I was frightened by her at first, but her happy cackling laugh and her obvious pleasure at seeing Grampy reassured me, and I did not cry when Grand-mamère held me on her knee, even though she smelled strongly of tobacco and sweat.

Once, when I had a new pair of shoes which I was proudly showing to Grampy, he told me about a pair of shoes he had gotten as a little boy of five or six himself. At the time Grampy and his family were traveling from the Gaspé to Old Town. It was in winter— maybe February—and they had been traveling by ox sled for days in the cold of eastern Canada and northern Maine. There were other families in the party, making a caravan of immigrants going to Old Town where there was work to be had in the huge pulp mill, and land to be had for farming. One day they came upon a herd of caribou, and the men in the party shot several. That night they ate very well, relishing the first meat they had eaten for days. From the skin of the caribou, Grand-papère had fashioned a pair of clumsy moccasins with leggings for Grampy, who had no shoes of his own to wear. Grampy told me how proud he had been of the boots his father had made. I wasn't sure what a caribou was, but for a long time I thought it would be nice to have a pair of caribou moccasins like Grampy's.

After his marriage, Grampy worked hard. He accumulated some land in Old Town, built a house for Dorilda, and they prospered, raising seven children. Grampy built a small business selling firewood and pulpwood, and bought more land. Dorilda coached him, taught him to write his name, and read the daily paper to him from front to back every day. She also read him books and taught him mathematics, a subject he understood instinctively. He became an independent "cruiser and scaler," assaying the standing lumber and pulpwood on various tracts of land for other landowners. He was very good at it, despite the fact that he carried all the figures in his head.

From the first week of their marriage, my parents spent most Sundays at Grandfather Pelletier's house. My grandmother expected it, because it was the custom of her culture. Father's brother Ed was also married and came with his wife, Flora. Mama and Dad were married in a double wedding with Edna, Dad's sister. For the first months of the marriage the two couples shared an apartment, and both couples returned on Sundays to the house on South Main Street in Old Town, where Dad and Aunt Edna's unmarried siblings still lived at home. I was the first grandchild, and when I came along, I went too, where I was greatly admired by all the family.

Grampy had a horse called Bob and a jigger wagon. Sometimes I would go with Grampy, seated high on the seat of the jigger, to carry wood to a customer. Often Grampy would give me the reins and let me drive. I'd hold them tight in my hands as Grampy instructed and say, "Gittup," or "Whoa" in a loud voice like

Grampy's. And when we got home, Grampy would take me into the kitchen and tell Grammy in French how I had driven Bob and how strong I was. Grammy was a no-nonsense woman who would cluck in good-natured disapproval at her husband's indulgence of me and then find us cookies or pie to eat.

At Grampy Pelletier's, French was the language of conversation. Everyone in the household spoke in French. At first Mama was put off by this, but the family really tried to remember that she did not understand French and gradually spoke more English in her presence.

What Mama found more difficult was the amount and volume of the French. The Pelletiers were exuberant. While both the parents spoke in moderate tones, the offspring spoke as if they were all deaf. Perhaps it was because Flora, Ed's wife, whose father was stone deaf, had a nice voice but used it at full volume. The others seemed to be trying to out-shout her.

On Sundays the Pelletiers gathered right after mass and stayed for the day. Grammy loved to cook, and was a truly great chef. Sunday dinners were held in the family dining room where the oak table—which could be extended four extra feet—literally groaned with the dishes of food Grammy cooked.

Dinners were served at noon and lasted for two hours. Once the grandchildren became numerous, they were seated in a row on one side with the women across the table. Grampy and Grammy sat at the head and foot of the table. Aunt Edna always served.

Dinners started with soup—chicken, vegetable, or pea. The soups were rich and tasty meals by themselves and the men sometimes ate two large bowlsful. Ed and Ray were huge men—Ed weighed over 300 pounds and Ray over 250. Dad was smaller, but ate prodigiously for his size.

Aunt Edna was a large woman, and the three unmarried aunts tended towards plumpness. All liked to eat and did so with gusto. My mother and Flora at first barely ate, but in time succumbed to the urging of the family and increased the amounts they, too, ate.

After the soup, the serious eating began, punctuated by continuous loud talk. There was always a huge roast of beef, lamb, pork, or in the fall venison, which was called simply "deer meat." Frequently there was roast chicken, chicken and dumplings, or Grammy's specialty, pork chops and dumplings. Several times a year there was turkey, and Christmas ensured an enormous goose. Much of the meat was raised by Grampy, who had a small farm on the property.

Vegetables were much a part of the menu—sometimes as many as six different ones to a meal. In season Grammy made tiny, glazed carrots, just two inches long, flavored with pure maple syrup. She made sweet pickled beets, rich in cinnamon and cloves. One of her recipes is a favorite with my children today: a cabbage dish made with cabbage diced to one-inch-sized pieces, and cooked with diced green peppers, scallions diced with their tops, and diced celery with its tops. This dish was cooked with a minimum of water and flavored with salt pork. We also ate rutabaga, mashed with brown or maple sugar added along with scads of butter.

Other vegetables such as cauliflower, broccoli, Brussels sprouts, and a variety of squashes all found their way to Grammy's table in special recipes she concocted. No meal was complete without a variety of homemade pickles and sauces.

And just when we thought we could eat no more, the family then attacked the desserts. Her fruit and berry pies captured the essence of the fresh fruit and emitted that essence with every mouthful of pie. Custard and cream pies were three inches deep with meringues and whipped cream.

Grampy, who was diabetic and not on insulin, ate a limited meal, specially prepared for him, with no sugars and somewhat limited starches. I never heard him complain even once, nor did he cheat on his regimen. He ate his rather plain meals with his gentle smile, always complimenting Grammy on his portions while the others gourmandized. Grampy's only dessert was Jello, which he ate with skimmed milk meal after meal. Yet he joined in the conversation in his quiet voice, often quieting the talk as he launched into some story of long-ago Canada.

At those times we all listened, even the children in the kitchen, who would come in and gather by their respective parents while Grampy talked. Sometimes Grammy would tell stories, too, but they were always of Grampy and of the early years of their marriage when Grampy spent the long winters in the North Woods in the lumber camps.

She must have been lonely and hard pressed to care for the livestock by herself during those years, but she only told of how hard it was for Grampy. Grampy had a slight accent and would end his stories in English with, "You Mamère, she is very good farmer. I am lucky man, me, for marry her," and we would all laugh and go back to the loud talk.

Whenever Grampy spoke of his winters in the North Woods and the ensuing springs when he came out of the woods with the long log drives down the West Branch of the Penobscot, all his sons listened attentively. Ed and my father had worked the river drives as boys, but by that time the drives were of pulpwood and not as exciting as the long log drives that Grampy knew.

Grampy told of the long evenings in camp, of sleeping in a single bed with twenty other men under one huge blanket, and of a diet of yellow-eye peas baked with molasses and salt pork three meals a day for days on end. Grammy would nod her head and in French attest to his hardship, sometimes with tears in her eyes.

And he told of the workday, which began on the job at dawn and ended at dark in bitter cold, sometimes waist-deep in snow. Grampy felt lucky to have earned the job as cruiser, going out to mark the trees other men would cut, often walking endless miles on snowshoes, cruising and hunting caribou for the camp. We all listened.

Although Grampy spoke in his French accent and had the least formal education, he was a wise and loving man. And while he could not read, he listened carefully while Grammy read him the paper each day and to the books she read aloud. He had a good grasp of world affairs and thought deeply about what he learned.

After our evening meals, the men adjourned to the living room where we listened to Grampy's radio. It was an upright RCA with push-button tuning. He was proud of his machine and listened to it by the hour, listening to the news commentators, especially H. V. Kaltenborn. Grampy had a great sense of humor and loved Jack Benny—perhaps because he worked for Jello. To my delight, Grampy also liked the children's programs of late afternoon: "Jack Armstrong," "Tom Mix," and "Little Orphan Annie." Thanks to him, I got my secret decoder pin because he bought me Ovaltine just so I could get the box top. We decoded many secret messages together. He was in awe of the decoder and really thought the messages exciting (even if they said, "Be sure to drink your Ovaltine").

Grampy and Grammy presided over the family and dinners, but quietly, kindly, with no direct commands. Their presence was like that of royalty, dictating the decorum and controlling the family group skillfully in conversation and mood. At these gatherings family values were learned by osmosis, almost, rather than by direct order. When disputes arose, which they did from time to time, it was Grampy or Grammy who arbitrated the dispute, quietly and firmly, with no appeal, but leaving each party thinking he or she had won. Sometimes disputes became quite heated, verging on anger, but no one ever went away from the gathering angry or holding a grudge. Grampy would not allow that. Through Grampy, peace reigned over the family. He taught each of us that tolerance is the key to goodwill, and we all felt his love.

2

Summers with Grampy

Every summer I spent two whole weeks with my Pelletier grand-parents in Old Town, across the bridge from Milford, where we lived. It was my summer vacation, they said. Dad had three younger sisters and a younger brother who still lived at home, and Aunt Edna and her husband and two children lived with Grammy and Grampy, too. The four bedrooms on the second floor were full to overflowing with the girls, and Uncle Ray, who had a room of his own. Grammy and Grampy had the big front bedroom, but Grampy seldom slept there, sleeping instead in the unfinished back chamber over the barn, because Grammy was often ill for long spells that confined her to her bed. My Aunt Edna and her husband shared a tiny bedroom off the kitchen with their two children. It was a crowded house, yet no one complained.

I loved my two weeks with my grandparents. I slept in Grampy's big iron bed in the back chamber. This room was open to the roof and had great screened windows that allowed the evening breezes to sweep through, clearing the room of any warm air. The walls were open studs which had been covered entirely with old playbills from the Strand Theater, or enormous calendars with pretty Gibson Girls on them. The playbills had pictures of Tom Mix, Buck Jones, and William H. Hart in full cowboy dress, riding spirited horses and with blazing guns in their hands. Just about all the movie stars of the '30s were pictured on the walls. It was a grand room to sleep in, especially as Grammy let me stay up until 9:00 or 9:30 and did not insist that the light be out when I did go to bed. I would lie in the big iron bed and read the movie posters or thumb through the old calendars looking up the days of past birthdays in my family.

The room was lit by a solitary light bulb that dangled from a twisted cord over the foot of the bed. The bulb was unfrosted and looked like a large radio tube with its heavy wiring clearly visible and orangy-yellow light accenting the colors of the playbills. The bulb had a sharp point on the top end that seemed to make it more exotic. A string attached to the bedpost ran to the chain pull on the socket that allowed me to turn the light off from the bed. I turned the light on and off many times after I discovered that the wires glowed eerily in the blackness above the bed just after I pulled the light chain.

Grampy worked from 3:00 to 11:00 P.M. every day as a crossing attendant for the Maine Central Railroad, and there were many nights when I would still be awake when Grampy got home at 11:30. I would hear the trolley stop in front of the house and know that Grampy was home. He would come quietly up the back stairs and feign surprise and consternation that I was still awake. Grampy slept in long underwear that he wore summer and winter. He would get into bed next to me smelling slightly of horses, bay rum, and sweat. It was an aroma that I didn't mind, for it enveloped me in the protective custody of Grampy's strength and maleness, and we would lie back-to-back in the darkness.

Many nights Grampy went to sleep immediately, but on others he would talk to me, telling me stories of when he was a young boy and had gone into the great woods of northern Maine to work in the lumber camps for the winter, first as a helper in the bunkhouse and then as a woodsman himself. He told of felling the big spruce and pine, of the heavy winter snows, the long hours, and the excitement of spring when the men came out of the camps to bring the lumber down the Penobscot or Kennebec to the sawmills of Milford and Old Town. I listened, enraptured by the tales. And Grampy would always end the stories with, "Now we go for sleep. You remember this. You grow up and learn good in the school. You go to university and learn big things. You very good boy, Franny." And he would kiss me tenderly on the forehead.

When morning came, I would wake to find that Grampy had once again slipped with the silence of a swimming fish from the bed, leaving me to sleep late. I would hurry to dress to seek out my grandfather, but Grammy would be waiting for me with my breakfast. Grammy insisted on breakfast, making piles of crepes and sausage with maple syrup, oatmeal and toast, and milk tea. Not until breakfast was eaten was I free to go.

Grampy had a schedule for his day. In the cool hours from six to nine he worked on his woodpile at the top of the garden. There were nearly thirty cords of firewood there at all times. Grampy had a woodlot over in Hogtown, where he cut trees for firewood for his house and to sell. By summer there was only splitting to do, which Grampy did expertly with his special splitting axe. He would swing the axe high over his head to bring it down into the log, cleaving it in one stroke. Sometimes a log with a large knot or burl would resist Grampy's axe, forcing him to render further strokes. If the log persisted in its stubborn behavior, Grampy would reach for the maul and wedges—a drastic cure for recalcitrant logs. A battle would ensue between man and log. Grampy always won, but the victory was a hollow one. He felt that using a maul was tacit admission that he was not a skillful axeman.

By nine the garden would be dried of the night's dew. No weed lived long in Grampy's garden. He searched them out daily with his hoe, ripping them from the soil and carrying them to the chicken pen to toss them over the fence. I helped, but my favorite task was picking potato bugs. Grampy detested potato bugs and picked them once a day, putting them in a can of kerosene. He then fired the kerosene, consigning the potato bugs to the hellish flames he thought they deserved. The bugs crackled and popped in the flames while I watched in glee.

As we worked in the garden, Grampy patiently pointed out to me the various differences of his vegetables, explaining the virtues and vices of each variety. I listened and learned willingly, proud of my grandfather's acceptance of me as an equal in the garden. Grampy's English gave some strange twists to the names of the vegetables. He talked of "temmy toes," his "carrups and beeps," and his stand of "happle trees," but I understood and did not try to correct his pronunciations.

Just before dinner, eggs were collected from the thirty or so hens in the coop. Most of the hens laid in the morning, announcing their latest egg with loud and raucous cackling. Before the eggs were collected, scratch feed was strewn, fresh water put in the water cans, and the feedbins filled with mash. Grampy was on a first-name basis with all his Rhode Island Red biddies, catching them and showing me their special characteristics close-up. Then the eggs were collected—large, brown eggs with thick shells enveloping the goodness of the yokes and whites inside. Sometimes Grampy would deftly crack an egg with one hand and swallow the contents raw.

After a hearty dinner at the kitchen table where all assembled each noon, Grampy and Grammy retired to the sun porch glider, where they sat side by side while Grammy read the *Bangor Daily News* to Grampy. She read all the front page, the local news of Old Town, and the editorial page in part. She read in English, but she spoke in French, making it easier for Grampy to understand. Grampy usually dozed off before the reading was finished, and Grammy let him sleep until two. At that time he would waken, go to the bathroom to wash, and ready himself for his work at the flag gate at three o'clock.

I waited at the trolley stop with Grampy and sometimes would go on the trolley to Parlin's Drug Store, where Grampy got off with me. I would get ten cents from Grampy to take the next trolley back home. That was a fun trip.

After I finished eighth grade, the vacations stopped. I had grown big enough to get a job with the town highway department that year. In the meantime, my relationship with my grandfather deepened. During the fall and winter, the Strand Theater had Wednesday night Westerns and give-away nights. Merchants in town gave tickets with purchases in their stores and provided raffle items. The numbers were drawn between the first and second showing. Bicycles, dish sets, and radios were the prizes. We went early every week, using the free passes from the store.

Grampy and I would go to the movies on Wednesday evenings while Dad minded the flag gate for Grampy. The theater was only five minutes from the gate, an easy walk. Grampy loved the Westerns and the cartoons and shorts. Of those, Mickey Mouse and Laurel and Hardy were Grampy's favorites. I read for him any captions that showed up on screen. Grampy bought us each a box of popcorn, which we munched on through the movie. Back at the flag station after the show, we would regale Dad with a complete recasting of the movie. There were many of these wonderful Wednesday evenings.

After I started high school in Old Town, the flag station was a frequent stop for me. Grampy still worked every day from three o'clock on, and was at the station when I got out of school in the afternoon. Several times a week I would stop and chat with him in the little station. There were an average of five trains a shift, requiring less than ten minutes of actual work for each train. The rest of the time was waiting time, leaving lots of time to sit and talk. Sometimes I would read from my school books, explaining all that I had learned on a given subject, and Grampy would nod his head and exclaim in wonder at some of the things I had learned. Grampy was a good student, I found. There was little that we talked of or read that he didn't remember.

During these visits I discovered that while my grandfather could not read, he was very skilled in basic math and could do problems in his head that I struggled with on paper. Grampy could add long columns of numbers in his head almost as fast as I could give the numbers. He was equally adept at multiplication and division, often helping me with math problems that I read to him. He couldn't always explain how he came up with the right answers and was almost embarrassed at my awe of his ability, saying in a deprecating way that he wasn't very smart, since he couldn't read. But I thought my grandfather was one of the smartest men I knew.

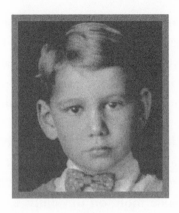

3

FIRST COMMUNION

By the time I was eight years old, God was often on my mind. I went to church regularly every Sunday morning and to catechism every Sunday afternoon. Dad and Mama also went to mass, and several times a year they attended special holiday services and all the Lenten services. Dad took me with him to special evening novenas where interminable prayers were said in French, and though I would get sleepy, Dad kept nudging me awake. Sometimes the nudging failed, and I would get a scolding on the drive home.

I really hated going to church. I hated the church building itself, the fake marble columns, the cracked and peeling figures, the grime and wear. I could see the serenely weathered faces of widows wearing rusty weeds, kneeling in somber piety while they recited their rosaries with silently moving lips. Old men, clasping their rosaries, joined them in prayer, noiselessly ticking off each decade of Hail Marys as the beads passed between thumb and forefinger. Their piety and devotion seemed real and deep, but I felt no such faith.

So I approached my First Communion with mixed feelings. Dad, especially, seemed elated by the prospect, admonishing me that it was a very important time in my life and that I must listen care-

fully to the priests and sisters in the special First Communion classes I attended every Saturday that spring. At the Lenten evening
rosary sessions that year, I offered silent supplications to God and to
the Virgin that I would be struck with true belief, that enlighten-
ment would descend on me, and that I would learn to love the
Church and God.

After each session of the rosary, I would feel that my pleas had
been heard, and elation would flood over me like a tidal wave. Then,
like the wave, the high emotion of the moment would recede, and I
would find myself once more on the shifty sandy beach of doubt.
Sometimes the elation would last until bedtime, when I would kneel
and recite all my prayers with great piety, being especially careful to
enunciate each word of the Hail Mary, Our Father, and Apostle's
Creed—and being especially careful with the Confiteor so that God,
if He was listening, would know that I had finally really found Him.
Sadly, it never lasted until morning.

Sometimes I tried to test God. Once I ate a piece of salami on
Friday, gingerly masticating the first bite for as long as I could before
swallowing. If thunder began rumbling in the heavens, I could spit
out the offending red meat and be spared the lightning bolt about to
be hurled by a wrathful God. When nothing happened, I kept eating.

In communion classes, I listened carefully but found no joy in
the words, no elation, no faith. On our several practices, when the
class went to the altar to receive unconsecrated hosts, I hoped the
taste of the bread would somehow be the taste of faith, but only
tasted disappointment.

But there were a few aspects of First Communion that I liked.
I would get a new blue serge suit—my first—and all new things to
go with it. Grampy and Grammy Pelletier were very happy their first
grandchild was making his First Communion and were buying me
a new white shirt, a tie, and new black shoes. Everyone in the family would be at mass to see me make my First Communion, and
there would be a party afterwards, with gifts.

I knew what the gift would be. New communicants always
received the same gifts. I'd get a tiny missal, a very nice rosary in a

little case, a scapula medal, and a little silver pin that said, "First Communion, 1933." But if I was really lucky, all my aunts and uncles would lavish me with other gifts more to my liking. Some might even be cash.

The missal would be a big problem. It wasn't something I really wanted, but I knew I would be expected to cherish it since it would be embossed in gold with my name and would come from Grammy Pelletier. I would be expected to carry it to church forever, and even worse, to use it from now on to follow the Mass. I would have to suffer my fate with it for long enough to be able to lose it with impunity, even with sympathy that I had lost something I valued so highly. That would take time.

But the bigger problem was the scapula. I would be expected to wear this emblem of my piety and faith around my neck as a symbol to the world. Most of the time my clothes would hide it from my many friends from the Milford Congregational Church, but summer was approaching and swimsuits offered no such concealment. I would have to be crafty.

Our communion ceremony was practiced for a week under the watchful eyes of the nuns. I learned to stand, kneel, and sit to the clack of the ebony blocks that Mother Superior kept in her hands. My only reprimand came from Sister Mary Christopher, who admonished me to lower my eyes to the floor while parading to the altar rail. She made me walk from my pew to the rail three times before she was satisfied that my mien exhibited a properly prayerful expression of repentance and faith. She also corrected my hands, showing me exactly where they should be on my chest, insisting that thumbs be tightly aligned to fingers as my palms were pressed together. I withstood the instruction with grim determination to survive the ordeal and a private oath that someday I would free myself of nuns forever.

On the last instruction Saturday, I was faced with the most dreadful part of my First Communion. I must make my first confession. Confession, also, had been practiced during the instruction lessons. I knew the prayers very well, but confession itself was a hateful idea. I didn't mind admitting to God in the privacy of my heart that I did sinful things sometimes, even though the seven deadly sins I had learned about seemed terribly distant from my life. But I tried to categorize my own sins by giving each one its proper name from the seven. I wondered uneasily if I was trying hard enough. When I asked Father Rivard what lust was, the good priest had seemed quite indecisive and evasive, finally answering that lust led to fornication and adultery, which were very bad sins indeed.

While I wasn't sure I had lusted enough to be a fornicator or adulterer, I thought I should probably admit to lusting a little, just to be safe. I had no trouble at all with lying. I knew I was a good liar. I could admit to at least a thousand lies in my eight years. And cursing and swearing were sins I was good at, too. I could think of lots of those words; I could even practice a little just before confession just to keep them in my mind and be current in my need for confession.

I just hoped I got to confess to Father Rivard. Some of the convent school kids who should know said that Father Lugger-knecht often gave the whole rosary as penance, while Father Rivard gave five Hail Marys at most. Of course, I could skip most of the penance and confess this omission at my next confession, but I wasn't sure what kind of sin that was. Sin could get terribly compli-cated. It was hard to do sin right.

As it turned out, my confession was to Father Rivard, who smiled when I confessed to lusting several times and nodded grave-ly at the amount of lying I admitted to. He admonished me about lying in the future. I also confessed to stealing nickels from Mama's pocketbook and was told that I must tell her what I had done. I promised to do that and kept quiet about the dimes. The next time I confessed, I would just say "money." I thought seriously about con-fessing to a little fornication, but decided against it until I had more experience with confession.

Father Rivard gave me three Hail Marys and an Our Father, which I thought was pretty stiff, but then I thought of the lifetime of sins I had committed and probably forgotten. It wasn't that bad after all. I said them all and felt quite good.

The first Sunday in June was the appointed Sunday, and it was a beautiful day. Dad got the entire family to church early for the lining up of the communicants outside on the steps. Proud parents crowded the grass by the succession of steps that led up to the huge renaissance doors of the church. Nuns in their starchy black and white habits herded their charges under the watchful eyes of Mother Superior. The girls in their white dresses and veils all giggled endlessly and fussed with their tiny bouquets, while the boys in their blue serge suits fidgeted and looked embarrassed about the white satin armbands on their left arms.

Father Luggerknecht arrived with Father Rivard to walk among the children and to beam on them in what he supposed was a happy smile, but which we were sure was a tacit threat that our behavior better be exemplary. Father Luggerknecht was an Alsatian who looked and acted like a Prussian drill sergeant in the Army of the Kaiser. He was about fifty years old with red-tinged, iron-gray hair cut in a severe military crop. He had no eyes, only a huge wrinkle of flesh that served as a bridge for his nose and in which there were slits where eyes should be. His mouth extended from jug ear to jug ear and opened into a cavity surrounded by enormous yellow teeth. His red and freckled face was the face of a Toby jug, squat and ugly, and sat directly on his shoulders, which were broad. His chin seemed screwed into his torso. Although he tried to project a jolly image, every child in the parish feared Father Luggerknecht, although no one could say why.

Father Rivard, on the other hand, was loved by each of us. He was tall, very thin, with lank black hair. He had a long, thin face but he smiled beautifully with his mouth and his eyes. It was a gentle, sad-sweet smile that came incongruously to his face, but extended downward to his heart. While Father Luggerknecht was the epitome of priestly satorical aplomb, Father Rivard wore patched and ragged soutanes that were close to being sackcloth and ashes. But he walked in grace. I loved Father Rivard and felt sure that he had some secret knowledge that he would impart to us children.

The lines were formed at last. Parents streamed inside to find seats on the aisles so they could see their child as he or she marched with downcast eyes to the rows of pews near the altar, reserved for the occasion. The organ pealed from the loft, filling the church with triumphant musical strains to which the choir added words of jubilance as we followed the priests and acolytes down the center aisle behind the crucifix and incensors. Dust rose in clouds, despite the sexton's careful sweeping the previous day, settling on the blue serge suit of each communicant boy as if drawn by magnetic threads woven into the fabric.

At our assigned pews, we stood in holy stances, hands together with fingers pointing toward heaven, and awaited the priests' entry to the altar. Then the sharp clack of the ebony blocks, and we all sat—girls on one side of the aisle, boys on the other. The Mass began, and we brought out our new missals to follow it. Angels hovered almost visibly over the heads of the girls, not so visibly over the boys.

At the break in the mass for the homily, Father Luggerknecht rose to the pulpit and my heart sank into my new knickers. I had hoped for Father Rivard, whose homilies were much shorter. It would be a long sermon, delivered in French. Bad French, Dad always said, because, according to Dad, Father Luggerknecht was almost as German as the Kaiser had been. But all that made no difference to me; I would suffer even if the homily had been given in English.

I turned my attention to the paintings in the altar apse. The gilt trim had hundreds of curlicues and I let my eyes trace them as I daydreamed the sermon away. The domed apse had been painted to look like the heavens opening to allow the cherubim to fly down to the waiting earth below, where a multitude gazed upward in reverent awe at the spectacle of God and cherubim. I thought idly that God looked more like Father Time than God, except that he had no scythe and was a tad too fat. Then I wondered whether the cherubim were boy cherubim or girl cherubim, and smiled slyly as I thought about lifting the filmy dresses they wore to find out what kind they were. But maybe angels were like the mannequins in clothing stores, and didn't have anything. That would be an awful way to be. I'd almost rather be a girl than an angel, if that were true.

Father Luggerknecht had droned on for thirty minutes of agonizing French when he finally closed the missal and descended from the pulpit. I came out of my reverie over angels and prepared for the finale of the morning. The consecration took place on the altar. The host was raised high as the little bells chimed, and all knelt. Mother Superior's ebony blocks clacked loudly, and we all obeyed their calls. Now the priest turned and held the host for the congregation to see, then descended the altar to march to the rail.

Mother Superior rose and the sharp clack of the blocks was heard again. We rose in unison, hands together in pointed humility, and stepped towards the altar railing to kneel. The girls received first, as the boys stood waiting. Father Luggerknecht started delivering the wafers to each waiting tongue while he murmured the Latin prayers. Each girl rose after receiving her wafer and returned with downcast eyes to her seat and a boy took her place at the altar.

The ceremony went without a hitch. Mother Superior beamed. I stole a glance at her as I returned to my pew. She really could smile! Parents glowed. The cherubim above the girls flew in circles, diving and twirling in celestial glee. Those over the boys smiled broadly and did a few sedate loops. The organ soared into the recessional, and the priests descended from the altar to pass to the front of the church in exultation at the completion of the Mass and the bringing of new souls to the sacrament of communion. We rose with our angelic guardians and followed.

Outside, pandemonium ensued. Parents gathered their children, heaping praise, hugs, and kisses on them. Kodaks snapped benignly at clusters of families surrounding a posing child. It was a happy day, and I reveled in all the attention.

First Communion hadn't been that bad after all. I had a nice new suit, and I would enjoy the party later, but I was nagged by the knowledge that I had none of the grace that Father Rivard and Sister Mary Christopher said would come with my First Communion. But maybe God wasn't someone I could find by engaging in a ritual, even though the ritual had been designed to please God.

4

A Capital Trip

In the summer of 1934, Tommy's father Loren invited me to go along with him and Tommy on a trip to Augusta. Tommy was my best friend. Loren Johnston was the town tax collector that year and needed to attend to town business at the state capital. I was thrilled at being asked to go along and worried at first that Dad would say no. Dad and Loren were not exactly friends. It bothered me that Dad didn't like Loren, because Loren was always nice to me and sometimes even seemed more interested in what I thought and did than Dad did. Dad was always very polite to Tommy, but I always had the feeling that he would have liked him even better if he had been anyone's son but Loren's.

Loren was aware that Dad didn't really like him much, and he used to twit Dad in little ways, sometimes suggesting that Dad stop walking around on his knees and stand up so that people could see him. Or he would say that Dad was pretty decent for a French Canuck. Dad took the jibes with a smile and would retort that he couldn't expect different behavior from a Yankee Ku Kluxer and Pee Eye, referring to Loren's distant Prince Edward Island ancestry. That they both held my Uncle Ray in high regard probably kept things from going further.

The day of our trip finally arrived and I rose early to dress in my Sunday best and present myself at Tommy's door by seven. Dad had given me last-minute instructions on being on my best behavior, along with fifty cents for lunch in Augusta. Mama had secretly increased my lunch money with a quarter, saying that I could use whatever I had left over from lunch to buy myself a souvenir of Augusta. I felt quite rich, but I was just a tad worried about eating in a restaurant. I never had, and I wondered if I could manage to eat with all those strangers watching me.

We left promptly a little after seven in Loren's green and black 1929 Chevrolet sedan. Tommy and I rode in the back seat so that we could each have a window. It was a three-hour drive to Augusta, and every mile was interesting as we ticked off the farms and towns. Loren took the road through Hampden to China Lake, which was a rather hilly road and had many delightful "Yes, Ma'ams" in it, which Loren made the most of, giving us some real thrills.

We stopped in Unity at Smiley's General Store while Loren got a pack of Camels. He bought us each a whoopee pie and a bottle of soda. I got an orange Nehi and Tommy got a Cliquot Club gingerale. We drank them slowly, after fizzing them as much and as often as we could.

The store owner was a genial man and inquired where we were headed. When we said we were going to Augusta to visit the state house, the store owner said, "While you're there, I wish you'd go up to the governor's office and tell the sonovabitch that if he don't get the road fixed and the turn widened on the side of Unity towards China Lake, Wesley Smiley is gonna come down to Augusta and personally kick his arse right up between his ears. The governor comes from over Dexter way. Lots of Branns over there. Louis J., he come looking for votes two year ago to get elected governor and making us all kinds of promises to fix our roads and stuff, and we ain't seen hide nor hair of the bastard since he went to Augusta. You boys tell him that for me. Here, have a banana caramel sucker so's you'll remember. Tell him Wesley sent you. He'll know who Wesley is, damn well enough."

Tommy and I stood wide-eyed while Wesley delivered his broadside. We accepted the suckers, tacitly agreeing to give the governor Wesley's message. Wesley then turned to Loren.

"You got business with the governor in Augusta? Take these boys in to see him with you. You tell 'em Wesley Smiley sent you and you'll get in to see him. Him and me go back a long ways. Lou stops here all the time when he's traveling around these parts. You tell him. Take those boys of your'n with you. Be good for them to see the governor."

Loren laughed and said he'd see if he couldn't make the time to see the governor, and we left with Wesley escorting us to the door, all the time exhorting us to use his name and "see the governor." Back in the Chevrolet, Tommy asked if we had to go see the governor and give him Wesley's message. Loren said we should wait until after he had finished his business with the state treasurer, and then we would try to see the governor. In the meantime, we should watch for the road and turn so that we would know what we were talking about.

We thought that was a good idea. We had scarcely cleared the village limits when we came on the curve that was clearly the one Wesley referred to. It skirted the end of a small marshy pond in a sharp arc that reached around for nearly 150 feet of washboardy broken pavement that sent the sedan skidding sideways as dust roiled up from under its wheels. Loren wrestled the wheel grimly and muttered, "No wonder Smiley wants this road fixed. Ain't safe to drive a hayrick over, let alone a car." We bounced around in the back seat, gleefully admiring the cloud of dust behind us and encouraging Loren to make as much as possible.

From Unity it was still an hour to Augusta. It was getting quite warm, and China Lake looked very cool and tempting. Loren said that China Lake was pretty, but that we wouldn't have time to go swimming. We saw several sailboats on the lake, sailing hull down in a stiff breeze, going fast. We had seen motorboats on the river, but had never seen sailboats before. When I said that I would like to sail a sailboat and sail against the wind, Tommy snorted in disgust, saying, "Sailboats have to sail where the wind blows them. You can't sail against the wind. Any dummy knows that."

I had just finished reading *The Eagle Scouts at Sea* and tried to explain about tacking downwind, but Tommy wouldn't listen until his father said from the front seat, "Tommy, shut up and listen to what Franny is saying. He's right. You can sail against the wind if you know how and have the right kind of boat. Don't be such a know-it-all."

Tommy sulked for a while, but then we were entering Augusta and the new sights soon cheered him up. We were both eager to see the capitol dome first and vied for positions at the windows. I spotted the dome first but kept quiet until Tommy let out a whoop of, "There it is!" I didn't care if Tommy got the glory, just so he got over the sulks.

We thought the grounds of the capitol were the most beautiful we had ever seen. There was nothing as grand in Bangor, not even the fairgrounds. Even the parking area was impressive, with little signs with names and titles on them for Augusta officials. After we parked, we ran around looking at the signs and the cars. We were disappointed that the spot marked for the governor contained a rather shabby-looking Hudson touring car which seemed unbefitting the governor of the great State of Maine. It did have the nice feature of a windshield between the front and rear seats and a siren on the right front fender.

The ground floor of the capitol was given over to a kind of museum of Maine wildlife, with stuffed fauna in every corner. Loren left us here with instructions not to stray from the building and to meet him at noon under the clock at the entry.

Left to our own devices, we wandered looking at everything. I particularly liked the stuffed moose family, although the papa moose seemed a little hidebare at the hindquarters and was standing in riffles of moose hair that curled around his rear hooves. The calf was in pretty good shape, though, and stood nursing alongside mother moose, who was posed with a look of serene maternal bliss. The entire tableau was displayed in a huge circular glass enclosure at the very center of the museum, and we lingered to admire it from all angles.

There were other exhibits that we admired, particularly the beaver lodge that was split in half so that we could see inside. We knew of a beaver dam and lodge at Third Stream and had often wondered how the beaver got in and out of it.

The morning went by quickly, and Loren found us at noon entranced by the black bears. We were each eager to tell him what we'd seen, and he was a good listener, asking questions and commenting at times. But now it was time for dinner.

Back in the car, Loren drove us to downtown Augusta. It was a busy little city and we were wide-eyed at the bustle of businessmen and lawmakers on their way to lunch. We were lucky and found a parking space very close to J. J. Newberry's. The counter inside was jammed, but we found an empty booth and sat down. A waitress came and handed us each a menu. My heart began to pound as I scanned the menu, looking at the prices first. Under sandwiches I found several choices for fifteen cents and breathed a sigh of relief. But before I could order the egg salad that I had decided on, Loren asked, "You hungry, Franny? You and Tommy can order whatever you like. That Salisbury Steak Blue Plate looks awful good to me."

Tommy's eyes widened. "Yeah, Franny, let's have that. Look, you get corn on the cob with it, and we'll have pie à la mode after, and lemonade to drink."

I felt compelled to price out Tommy's order as he ran it off. The Blue Plate was ninety-five cents, the lemonade was ten, and the pie à la mode was twenty cents. The whole meal would cost a dollar and a quarter! I gasped at the amount and was about to say I'd have the egg salad when Loren said, "Don't worry about the cost, Franny. I know your father gave you some money, but you keep it to buy yourself a souvenir this afternoon. Get what you'd like to eat. I'll take care of your father if he says anything when we get home."

The waitress took our orders: three Blue Plate Salisbury Steaks with lemonade and apple pie à la mode. When my dinner arrived I was surprised to find that Salisbury Steak looked an awful lot like a hamburger patty, but after the first bite decided even if it was a hamburger, it was the best I'd ever eaten. There seemed to be bits of chopped red peppers in it, along with some onions and other stuff, but it tasted great. Loren put Worcestershire sauce on his steak and I followed suit, after Tommy mimicked his father and covered his steak in sauce. I applied the sauce sparingly, tasted the meat, liked it, and then added more sauce. It was the first time I'd ever eaten meat with Worcestershire sauce on it, and I thought it lent a pretty exotic note to dinner. I would have to tell Mama about it when I got home.

The dinner was good, although the ice-cream-scoop serving of potatoes seemed a tad small. I could easily have eaten two more scoops. And the apple pie wasn't as sweet as Mama's, but the crust was much better. All in all it was a good dinner, and once I started to eat, I had forgotten about the people around me and enjoyed my meal. I remembered to use the paper napkin the way Mama had told me, too. The best part, though, was when Loren handed us each ten cents to leave by our plates for a tip. "You always leave a tip for the waitress, especially if they serve good," he said, leaving a quarter beside his own plate. I thought the waitress must be rich to get forty-five cents for each meal she served!

Then Loren told us, "I have a few things to do. You boys can find a souvenir here in Newberry's or you can go down the street to Woolworth's. I will be an hour. If you get tired go back to the car and wait for me there, but don't be later than two o'clock. You can check on the time by the clock over the lunch counter. Don't get lost." With those instructions he left on his errands.

We headed for the toy department. This store was bigger than Woolworth's in Old Town and had a basement level, to boot. Toys were in the basement. Just by the top of the stairs, we saw the perfect souvenirs of Augusta. A counter with a big sign saying "Back to School Sale" was loaded with more school supplies than either of us could ever have imagined, and there in the middle were the prize items. A sign on the pencil boxes said, "Today only. Three-drawer pencil boxes, regularly $1.00, now 75¢." There were piles of the grandest pencil boxes I had ever seen. They came in four colors: red, blue, green, and yellow. Each had three drawers that pulled out to reveal that they were filled with everything a student would need.

The top tray had a ruler and eraser, four #2 pencils, a double-ended red and blue pencil, and a pencil sharpener. Then the first drawer had a protractor, compass, four short drawing pencils, and a tiny pad of tracing paper. The second drawer contained an assortment of sixteen wax crayons and sixteen colored pencils, plus a thin gum eraser. And the third drawer was the best of all. It was full of watercolor paints and had three brushes of varying sizes with a tiny instruction book on watercolors. It all fit in a box about five by ten inches, nearly four inches thick. The cover said "Maine-ly School Days," and underneath, "Souvenir of Augusta, Maine. Capital of the Pinetree State." The boxes were works of art.

We knew in an instant that we had found the souvenir of souvenirs. When our classmates saw us pull out such a box, we would be the envy of the school. The box contents were lavish beyond belief, and the box cover would proclaim to all who beheld it that the owner was a person who had seen the world, an adventurer who went to far-off places, who had visited the capital of the Pinetree State. It was a souvenir to be proud of—even venerated.

I had fished my fifty-cent piece and quarter from the depths of my pants pocket and held them clenched tightly in my sweaty fist while I waited for the salesperson to come my way. Despite the fact that there were at least a hundred boxes on the counter before me, I was struck by a great fear that none would be left for me before someone waited on me—such was my lust for a box. I had decided on a red one. Red was my favorite color, and this red was the reddest red ever seen.

From afar came a low voice that cleared the red mist clouding my vision. "Can I help you, Sonny?" A grandmotherly looking woman was behind the counter. She smiled at me through glasses like Grammy Spruce wore, tiny oval lenses in gold wire frames.

She looked kind of like Grammy, too, with whitish hair in a bun. "Did you want to buy something, Sonny?"

I pointed to the red pencil box. "I want to get one of them," I said. I didn't say "pencil box" for fear that it might be called by some other name because it was so grand.

"Oh, that's a nice choice. Red's a good color. Easy to see. That will be seventy-five cents, please." The lady reached for my coins with one hand and picked up an unopened box from the pile with the others. "What school do you go to? You must be in third grade at least," she ran on.

"I go to Mayhew School in Milford. Milford is a hundred miles from Augusta. We're visiting the capital and maybe we'll see the governor today." I found the words rolling from my mouth with ease.

The lady handed me my box, now in a paper bag. "Well, you are a long way from home! And going to see the governor! I've lived in Augusta all my life and have never seen the governor. This must be a good day for you. I hope you enjoy your schoolbox."

She waited on Tommy next, who chose a yellow box and had more conversation with her. Then we left Newberry's with our souvenirs, and went to find the car. We didn't have to wait long for Loren, whose business hadn't taken as long as he thought it would.

We showed him our boxes in great excitement, pulling out the drawers so that he could see and admire the contents. He told us we had certainly gotten our money's worth.

Then Loren said we needed to go back to the capitol building again. We were going to try to see the governor. He told us to speak up if the governor talked to us. It was quite warm now, and Loren had taken off his suit jacket but still wore his straw boater with the striped band. He also wore striped gaiters on his shirtsleeves. Loren was tall and rather thin, and I thought he was handsome. I figured the governor would see us for sure if we were with Loren.

Back at the capitol we took an elevator to the third floor and walked down a corridor to a room marked "Executive Suite." I didn't see any suit when we went in, only a very stern-looking woman behind a desk with a funny-looking headset on her head.

She was typing furiously and did not stop. Loren waited until she looked up.

"I'd like to see Governor Brann. I'm Loren Johnston, tax collector from Milford. I saw Lou at the Legion convention in Lewiston last month and he told me to call in the next time I was in Augusta. I want him to meet my son and his friend. He may need their votes someday."

The stern lady softened under Loren's warm smile. "Well," she said, "it's been a quiet day. I'll see if he can see you." She pushed a button on her desk and when a man's voice said, "Yes, Miss Carswell?" she said, "A Mr. Loren Johnston is here to see you, Governor. Shall I send him in?"

"Bring him in," the voice boomed over the speaker. Miss Carswell got up and ushered us to the door of the governor's office. It opened into a large room on the far side of which a desk was placed before a curved wall of windows that provided a fine view. The desk was flanked on each side by flags of the United States and the blue flag of the State of Maine. As we entered the governor rose from his chair behind his desk and came forward to greet us.

"Nice to see you, Loren. And I see you brought me some important visitors." He thrust his hand out to Tommy. "What's your name, Sonny?" he asked.

Tommy shook the proffered hand and replied, "Thornton Johnston, but everyone calls me Tommy."

"Well, Tommy, welcome to Augusta. I'll call you Tommy, too. This fellow here must be your father. I know your father pretty well from the American Legion, you know."

Then he turned to me. "And who is this young man?"

I gave my name, being careful to say that everyone called me Franny.

"Well, Franny, you and Tommy must be pretty good friends, I guess. You go to school? What grade are you in?"

Tommy was quick to answer. "We'll be in third grade when we go back to school in three weeks."

"That's fine. Now I tell you what I'm going to do. I'm going to give each of you a new lead pencil with my name on it so that you will be able to remember your visit here." The governor reached into the top drawer of his desk and brought out two shiny blue mechanical pencils, passing one to each of us. The pencils were the blue of the state flag and had the state seal embossed at the top with the words "Compliments of the Governor's Office, State of Maine" and the signature "Louis J. Brann, Governor" under them. Both of us said polite thank-yous. The governor beamed.

Then the governor turned his attention to Loren. "You got anything special needs attention up in Milford, Loren?" he asked.

"Nope, just thought I'd call in while I'm here. Had some business with the state treasurer that I took care of this morning. But the boys might have a little something for you. They got a message to deliver from Wesley Smiley, owns Smiley's Store in Unity Four Corners. What did Mr. Smiley ask you to tell the governor, Tommy?"

Tommy was very uneasy and blushed.

The governor helped him out, saying, "Go ahead, Tommy. I know old Wes from way back. He's always got an axe or two to grind. What's he want this time? You tell me just what he said."

Tommy swallowed, remembering Wesley's colorful message, then he spoke.

"He wants you to get the piece of road with the bad curve and washboardy tar fixed like it was promised. He said he didn't want to have to come down here and kick your behind [Tommy said bee-hind, not arse] up between your ears." Then Tommy smiled weakly while waiting to see what the governor's reaction would be.

The governor laughed loudly and slapped his thighs.

"That sounds just like old Wesley. Only I bet he used a lot more cuss words. I better see that the road gets fixed or no telling what the old reprobate will do, but it will be a cold day in hell before he's able to carry out his promise."

Then the governor turned to Loren. "These are pretty good youngsters you got here, Loren. Bring 'em around again next time you're down this way. You fellows study hard in school, and maybe you'll be unlucky enough to get to be governor yourself some day.

And you come again." With those words he ushered us all to the door.

The long ride home wasn't nearly as eventful as the one down. We stopped again at Smiley's Store, but Wesley had gone off to deliver a load of grain to some farmer in Troy. Loren treated us to another cold soda and an ice cream cone. We nursed our goodies all the way to Hampden Highlands.

I arrived home shortly after six that evening, a little late for supper but Dad never said a thing. He admired my pencil box along with the rest of the family and didn't tarnish my excitement by saying that I shouldn't have spent all that money. He only asked if I had been sure to say thank-you for lunch. While I ate my supper, everyone sat at the table and listened to how I had met the governor and eaten in a real restaurant.

When school started, the souvenir pencil boxes were admired greatly and the mechanical pencils that the governor had given us were objects of reverence, having been bestowed by a Head of State. It all made 1934 seem special, a year to remember.

5

THE LINDBERGH SUIT

Many of my friends had fathers who were out of work in 1934, which was a deep depression year. The woolen mill in Old Town had closed more than a year before and would never reopen as a woolen mill again. The Ounegan Mill still struggled but was on short hours. The pie plate factory was in dire distress, and even the pulp mill was breathing hard and had gone to six-hour shifts to spread the work around.

I was unaware of the economics of the times. I heard my parents and relatives speak of the "hard times," but poverty was not a word in my vocabulary, although the family struggled to make ends meet. Dad worked long hours in the store, coming home to longer hours in the garden or at the woodpile. Pennies were precious. One did not waste anything that could be used or re-used.

Mama sewed clothes for me and my family on the new Singer sewing machine that she and Dad were paying for at a dollar a month. The Singer was a source of great joy to Mama. She diligently made dresses and jumpers for Ellen and pajamas for me and for Paul. She made new clothes from old clothes handed down from friends, taking the old garments apart, pressing the pieces, and cutting and resewing them into serviceable, if not fashionable, garments for us.

While Mama liked to sew and make clothes, her efforts were not always appreciated by me. And in a way the joy of the electric machine was tempered by the need to use it. Mama became a slave of the Singer, spending long hours at it to ensure that the dollar-a-month payment was justified in Dad's eyes.

Mama was not a skilled seamstress. She could make wearable clothes, but only barely so. Ellen's dresses were her best effort, but they looked homemade despite Mama's most careful work. The boys' clothes were all disasters. Seams were lumpy and irregular, and her choice of fabric was dictated by what she had, not what would look right.

I was only dimly aware of my wardrobe deficiencies, but Ellen often cried at wearing some of the dresses. Paully accepted anything that Mama made with serene pleasure, wearing the creation proudly and showing it off to all who would look. Mama and Dad were struggling to provide warmth, shelter, and food for us all, and style and fashion were not a high priority on their agenda. Occasionally, though, Mama's efforts were inspired. Some greater power seemed to possess her and guide her fingers, and she'd produce a truly outstanding garment, worthy of pride of ownership.

In the fall of 1934 I entered third grade. I had grown rapidly that summer, outgrowing most of my meager wardrobe. The early fall months were no problem. I simply continued to go to school in my too-small short pants and a shirtwaist.

At that time young boys were still wearing little cotton suits of short pants that buttoned to a shirt with a row of buttons around the waist of the shirt. In warm weather ankle socks were worn, but as cold weather came the ankle socks gave way to long stockings reaching up to the thighs under the shorts, where they were fastened with garters attached to a garter belt worn over the underwear. The whole effect was both unsightly and uncomfortable, but children were forced to endure it.

After third grade boys graduated into knickers. These were longer pants with a cuff that made them blouse just under the knee. They were much more comfortable and hid the terrible garters. Many boys wore knee socks that required no garters at all, coming up over the cuffs on the pants. The socks had elasticized cuffs of their own into which the pants cuff was tucked. Young boys could scarcely wait to get into knickers.

Some parents insisted that their sons continue in short pants until a certain age or grade was attained. Dad was of this school of thought. He not only insisted on short pants, but he insisted that the proper hosiery for cool weather (in his mind any temperature below 72°F) should be black cotton stockings that reached far up my thighs. I hated them with a deep and abiding hatred. Unfortunately the store carried them in large quantities, they were almost indestructible, and they were cheap. Dad could not resist such a combination of favorable factors and decreed that they would be what I wore. No amount of pleading could change his mind. I wore black stockings.

So it was that in 1934 when I went back to school, Mama—to her credit—sided with me and argued with Dad that the few cents saved between black stockings and tan ones wasn't too great a price to pay to make me happy. She also told him that I had out-grown everything I owned and had to have new clothes.

Dad responded with the suggestion that Mama lower the buttons on the shirtwaists so that the pants would ride lower. I wailed that I couldn't walk in pants with the crotch at knee level, but Dad wasn't easily persuaded, especially if the clothes still had some wear to them. Money was tight, so I suffered through the fall in pants that made me hobble when I walked.

I had just about resigned myself to a long, cold winter in too-short, short pants, the hated black stockings, and the humiliating garters showing above my knees. I was saved from my despair by

Grammy Pelletier, who had returned from her annual visit to her sister in Torrington, Connecticut. We knew this was somewhere near New York City, because on one trip she had brought home little sparkler wheels that she said she purchased from a street peddler in New York City for five cents. On this trip, however, Grammy had been more practical. She returned with a supply of medium-weight woolen fabrics to be used to make clothing for her grandchildren. She also came loaded with many pairs of children's long underwear purchased as factory seconds from the factory in Torrington.

The fabric would make great winter pants, shirts, and jackets. There was only one drawback. It came in only two shades: a burnt orange and a nauseating shade of puce, a purplish-brown color that to my mind would only be a bargain if someone had paid Grammy a dollar a yard to take it.

From mid-October to Thanksgiving, Mama toiled at her machine while I protested at the many fittings and pinnings. Mama was determined to make me an entirely new wardrobe for my birthday on the day before Thanksgiving. My protests over the fittings were somewhat mollified by the fact that Mama had secretly conspired to make me knickers instead of short pants. But Mama was willing to go even a step beyond the knickers. She asked me if there was anything I would particularly like to have. She would make it for me for a special birthday present.

My hero of heroes was Colonel Lindbergh. I read avidly of his exploits and doted on anything pertaining to the great flyer. I especially admired the flying breeches, long coat, and goggles the flyer often wore in the newsreels. I thought the goggles were wizard and longed for a helmet of my own.

Tommy, my very, very best friend and confidante, lived with his Grandma Dunphy, who was the best seamstress in town. She had loads of pattern books that women would use to pick dresses from for her to make. In the Simplicity book I found a costume for boys that was a complete aviator's ensemble exactly like Lindbergh's. In fact, the pattern proclaimed it to have Lindbergh's stamp of approval as to its authenticity.

I borrowed the book from Grandma Dunphy and showed it to Mama, scarcely daring to hope that she might buy the pattern and attempt to make the clothes. Anyone could sew the pattern, the caption said. It added that any boy would love to wear the costume, a truism beyond a shadow of a doubt. Mama studied the picture, pursing her mouth as she read the requirements for fabric and thread. "Thirty-five cents is a lot of money for a pattern," she finally said. "Maybe Woolworth's won't have it in stock. We'll see."

Friday evening was shopping night for Mama and Dad. They went to Old Town. Sometimes they went together, and sometimes Mama went alone if Dad was working in the store. This Friday Mama went alone. On Saturday morning she told me I couldn't go out until she finished some fittings. I was indignant. Fittings on Saturday morning! Mama never sewed on Saturdays. She baked bread and beans, mended Sunday clothing for mass, and put clean sheets on all the beds. It wasn't until the bread was set to rise and the beans were in the oven that Mama called me for this hated fitting.

Mama sewed in the front room by the window where the light was better and where she could look out on the Penobscot River and see Indian Island. She loved the river and often said it was the world's prettiest river; I couldn't understand how she could compare it to other rivers she had never seen. This morning she stood me in the light of the window but instead of bringing out the usual unfinished garment, she produced the Simplicity pattern for the Lindbergh suit. "I have to try the pattern pieces to shorten them for you," she said. "I couldn't get your size. This one is larger."

Joy swelled in my bosom as elation blanketed my mind. I was really going to get a Lindbergh suit. The knowledge overwhelmed me. Now Mama was all business and efficiency. Usually when she sewed, she fussed and worried, pinned and tucked, and declared that she could never get things to come out right like the patterns said things should look. But this morning Mama had an air of professionalism about her that brooked no fears about her inadequacies as a seamstress. She plunged into the creation of a Lindbergh suit as though she were a professional tailor.

As she pinned and marked the pattern, she talked to me about the project. "Now we are going to surprise Dad. We're going to make the jacket and the breeches. We'll make the breeches from the puce-colored cloth that Grammy brought from Torrington. Aren't we lucky that aviator breeches are almost always that color? And we're going to make the jacket from the burnt-orange fabric. It will have a real fur collar from one of Auntie's coats. Aviators like colorful clothes so that they can be seen easily, and you know that Colonel Lindbergh's coat has a fur collar. If you are lucky, maybe Santa Claus will bring you a real artificial leather helmet and a pair of high lace boots for Christmas, like the ones you showed me in the Spiegel catalog. But you have to help me. I can't do it alone."

I instantly became a willing co-conspirator with Mama. The dreadful puce fabric suddenly seemed ideal for breeches, and the burnt orange just the material for the jacket. I had a vision of myself in the cockpit of the *Spirit of St. Louis,* fur collar raised against the wind and goggles down as I battled my way through the air over a great ocean liner while the passengers waved wildly from the decks below and I waved back nonchalantly (great flyers were always waving nonchalantly) from the cockpit. The passengers would remember me in my colorful attire forever and tell their grandchildren that they had seen the great flyer himself. Oh, it was going to be a great outfit! My new confidence in my mother's tailoring skills completely obliterated memories of past debacles.

Together, Mama and I worked on the Lindbergh suit and several pairs of knickers at the same time. It was impossible to keep the entire project from Dad's knowledge, so a program of limited information was used to feed Dad just enough to let him know that my wardrobe was in progress, without letting him know that I would soon be wearing knickers, not shorts. Nothing was said of the breeches, but Mama did venture to point out that winter was at hand and I would need new boots for the winter snow.

The picture on the pattern envelope pictured a flyer in high-topped leather logging boots like Dad wore, and, of course, I would need such boots to complete my outfit. Mama was paving the way for getting the boots. I already knew that such boots were available at the store. They came in two heights, eight-inch and twelve-inch. The twelve-inch boots had a pocket on the right boot containing a bone-handled pocketknife. I drooled over the boots each day at the store, where they were displayed in the dry goods section.

Tommy had been promised a pair of twelve-inchers for Christmas and was bragging just a little already. I told Mama about the boots, explaining that just plain gum rubbers wouldn't go with a genuine Lindbergh suit, especially if the wearer had a genuine artificial leather helmet with goggles to wear. Mama said, "Hmmm, we'll see what we can do," and began to prepare Dad.

Well, the Lindbergh suit was finally finished quite late on the eve of my birthday. It was a bitter cold night for November, and Dad was reading his *Argosy* magazine by the heater stove in the front room when Mama sewed the last buttons on the pants legs and the fly. She was just picking up the flight jacket in preparation for pressing it when Dad looked up and asked what she was doing. I was listening to Pick and Pat on the Dill's Best Pipe Tobacco show on the radio, but my heart wasn't with Pick and Pat that night. I was waiting for the Lindbergh suit to see it in its full completed glory.

"What are you sewing on, Fanny?" Dad asked Mama, as she stitched the buttons on the jacket front and pocket flaps. The jacket had four large patch pockets and a belt around the waist. The belt had a brass buckle with some intricate scrolling, salvaged from one of Auntie's gowns. No one would have guessed it, though, since it looked just like what an intrepid flyer would have.

Mama held up the nearly finished jacket. It lacked only the pocket buttons. "I'm just finishing Franny's Lindbergh suit. I made it from the material your mother brought from Torrington that you said I should use to make pants and things for Franny because he needs them pretty bad. I'm just about done on this Lindbergh suit, and the knickers are all done, but he has to have a pair of twelve-inch logger boots. Would you like to see him in his Lindbergh suit?" Mama spoke evenly and calmly, as if Dad knew all along that she was making the Lindbergh suit.

Some surprise showed in Dad's face, but he couldn't say he didn't want to see the Lindbergh suit since he had told Mama to make something for me from Grammy's fabrics. Mama held up the jacket. "This burnt orange is just the right color for a Lindbergh suit, don't you think? And these breeches set off the jacket real nice. The purple-brown looks real nice on Franny, and the breeches are nice and full in the seat and stand out good at the thighs. They just need the logger's boots to be authentic-looking. When Santa brings his helmet and goggles at Christmas, he should be very well dressed for the winter in good sturdy stuff. This Lindbergh suit will last two winters because it's pretty large for him. You'll see when he tries it on. Come try on your Lindbergh suit for Dad, Franny."

I didn't even wait for the end of Pick and Pat but left my place by the radio to do as asked. Dad was looking kind of gassed, like he'd swallowed something that had given him a sudden bilious attack. Mama brought out the knickers now, and, holding them up for Dad's approval, said, "Look how nice these knickers came out, Emile. I think I did a great job with the flies. And notice the little belts at the knees. They won't stretch like elastic cuffs, and they'll set off the tan or beige stockings very well." Mama was pressing her luck danger-ously now with talk of anything but black "Bear" brand stockings, but she knew when she had an edge, and she used her edge with the skill of an executioner showing no mercy.

In the meantime, I had donned the suit. It was a little big, but as Mama said, it would see me through two seasons and fit was a small price to pay for such an outfit. Dad appraised Mama's efforts. His gassy look dissolved into a smile of appreciation. Dad was a worker, people always said, and he knew good work when he saw it.

"Gosh, Fanny, that's a real spiffy-looking outfit." Then he turned to me, saying, "You ought to be happy to wear the clothes your mother made. She must have worked real hard. She's right, too. You do need logger boots to go with your Lindbergh suit, and we've got just what you need at the store. You better come down with me in the morning and pick out a pair you like. Wear your Lindbergh suit so Uncle Ray and Grampy Spruce can see how nice you look and how good Mama sews. The boots will be a birthday present from me."

The next morning at R. J. Spruce and Son I got fitted with a pair of dark brown logger's boots with a knife in the pocket. Grampy Spruce admired the Lindbergh suit, saying the colors were great for winter, and he gave me a whole dollar for a birthday present. Uncle Ray came out with a box that said "Utterback-Gleason Sporting Goods" and laid it on the counter. He opened the box and genuine artificial leather helmets and goggles spilled out. A size medium seemed to be just right, although the goggles were a little large and made me feel cross-eyed. But the helmet was warm and serviceable and would last two seasons.

It was a great birthday. One of the best I ever had. I wore my Lindbergh suit to school and was greatly admired in it. None of the kids knew it was homemade. No one would ever dream that such a suit could be. I wore my helmet with the goggles down during recess, even though they made me feel a little nauseous. The looks of envy on the faces of my friends were worth a little discomfort.

The Lindbergh suit lasted more than two seasons, but Mama proved to be a one-suit tailor. She never again made anything for me that was even half as good as the Lindbergh suit, but I didn't care. By then I'd learned that my clothes were beautiful and warm because they were sewn with stitches from the heart and lined with the fabric of love.

6

THE BIG SNOWSTORM

I had a love-hate relationship with snow. I passionately loved the snow for the rollicking joy of playing snow games and for the sheer beauty that snow and cold gave to the small New England town in which I lived. But I hated the snow with equal passion for the demands it put on me in shoveling endless walks and driveways, of working at the annual winter task of cutting firewood for the next year, and for the additional burdens it put on my daily chores.

The winter I was ten years old, we had a lot of snow, but the winter seemed no different than other winters except that from just before Christmas and on into the winter, my Grammy Pelletier was very ill. Christmas was held at her house, as usual. All of my aunts, uncles, and cousins gathered at the house on South Main Street in Old Town on Christmas Eve after midnight mass for the chicken soup and goodies that were a family tradition, but that year Aunt Edna did all the cooking. Grammy remained upstairs in bed.

The usually boisterous atmosphere had been muted to the point where we children were hushed with stage-whisper warnings that, "Grammy is sleeping" or "Grammy is awake." Even opening our presents was a hushed event. Loud screams of delight were taboo. In the afternoon on Christmas Day, one by one we were led up to Grammy's room to be presented to her. I was first because I was the first grandchild. She was ensconced in her big bed with the high wooden headboard, looking quite well, I thought. She sat propped up with lovely lacy pillows, wearing a frilly blue dressing gown that included some kind of matching bed bonnet of lace and ribbons. The curtains were drawn and the room was in semi-darkness with just the light of the bed lamps casting an orange aura over the bed.

I marched dutifully up to Grammy and gave her a kiss, as I had been told to do by my father. I didn't really like doing that, because Grammy's face was soft and doughy, like Mama's bread when she is kneading it. Also, while Grammy smelled of flowery perfumes, there was an under odor of mentholated medications that did not mix well with the floral scents. Grammy kissed me back weakly and asked in a faint voice if Santa had been good to me. Her hands grasped mine tenuously. They were dry and papery feeling and seemed much thinner than I remembered them. It was then that I noticed that her upper arm, which had always been full-fleshed and solidly strong when she held me on her lap, was now a drooping bag of wrinkled skin loosely filled with some articulated sticks of bones and stuff. It frightened me. I wanted to pull away, but I knew Dad would be angry with me if I showed my fright.

Grammy did not hold me long. Once she released my hand, I stepped back and she didn't object. She asked me a few more questions, then asked my aunt to hand over the purse that was on the foot of the bed. She fumbled through the purse with difficulty and withdrew a quarter, which she pressed into the palm of my right hand.

"Buy something you like at the Five and Ten. Anything you want," she said. Then, turning to my dad, "Emile, he's a good boy. Don't work him so hard and let him play more. He doesn't smile enough for a little boy," she continued. Then she seemed to collapse on the pillows and Dad took me out of the room. Grammy had cautioned Dad before about letting me play more. Every summer I spent two weeks at her house where she let me do just about anything I pleased. I was her first grandchild and she doted on me.

From that Christmas Day until mid February, I was taken every Sunday to see my grandmother and the scene was replayed each week. Even I could see that Grammy was getting weaker and more frail. Some Sundays she didn't speak at all, merely stared at me with half-closed eyes. Then we had the big snowstorm.

It started snowing while I was at church for Sunday mass. Dad had dropped me off with my sister and brother for the eight o'clock "Children's Mass" with instructions to go to our grandparents' home when mass was over. We did that often. It was a bitterly cold day. The snow had only just begun to fall when we arrived at the church, but the wind was blowing fiercely in hard, biting gusts. When mass was over, snow was falling in earnest, and we trudged the half mile to our grandparents' with heads down in the stinging snow. My younger brother Paul cried because his thumbs were cold and the snow was too deep for him. We were glad to arrive in the warmth of Aunt Edna's kitchen, where she fussed over us and scolded Dad and Uncle Ed—who were there, too—for not having gone after us with the car.

They both looked sheepish over their sister's scolding. My younger aunts joined Edna with some waspish jibes at the men. Aunt Dolores, who was a nurse and had been caring for Grammy, came into the kitchen and pursed her lips, covering them with a raised finger to shush the rising noise. I knew that something was wrong. All the faces were strained, and I realized that my younger aunts had been crying.

Grammy had taken a turn for the worse. None of us children was presented to her that day. The family all gathered as usual, but we sat in the kitchen, dining room, and living room in quiet little groups while Dolores and Aunt Edna frequently scurried upstairs. Outside the storm raged. Shortly before noon, Dad loaded us into the Model B and we departed, despite pleas from Aunt Edna to stay for dinner. The ride home to Milford was a slow one. There was now nearly eight inches of snow on the streets, and it was drifting badly in spots. No plows were out. Dad hunched over the wheel of the car, doggedly scraping frost from the windshield which was accumulating despite the new heater in the car.

We barely made it up the slight hill to our house. The tires spun and snow flew from them as the car fishtailed up the drive. We dashed into the house, all breathless and snowy, while Dad turned the Ford around to face the street. We knew that he expected a lot of snow when was parked the car like that.

Dinner was subdued. Afterwards Dad helped Paul and me fill the woodboxes by each stove, something he had never done before. The storm seemed to grow more fierce with each hour. Dad paced about, his face drawn and tight. Mama looked sad, and took us into the front room to read to us. It was a long afternoon.

Just before dark the storm abated somewhat. Dad was seated in his chair by the heater stove in the front room when he saw the state plow go by during the lull. He immediately got up.

"I think I had better go back to see Mother," he said to Mama. "Don't worry about me. If I get stuck, I will walk, and I will probably stay there overnight. There is plenty of wood, and you will be okay." Mama helped him with his mackinaw, cautioned him to be careful, and went to the door with him. We children stood around in awe, knowing something was wrong but unsure of what. We watched as Dad got the Ford going and drove off into the dusk.

As soon as Dad left, Mama gathered us around her and told us that Dad was going to stay with Grammy because she might be going to live with the angels. It was a solemn occasion, but none of us was frightened. Paul was mildly curious as to how Grammy would get to where the angels lived in the storm and was happy with Mama's explanation that when you went with the angels, you got wings just like they had. None of us worried about Dad being out in the storm. After all, Dad was strong and could do anything.

Dad did not come home until noon the next day. The storm ceased around breakfast time, after depositing twenty inches of fluffy, dry snow. Paul and I started shoveling the drive at Mama's suggestion and had made a path to the sidewalk by the time children on the street were passing on their way to school. We joined them, delighting in the deep snow of the, as yet, unplowed sidewalk. At the top of the hill we met Sam Sleeper with his horse Jim pulling the town sidewalk plow, and we hitched a ride halfway back home before old Sam made us get off and go to school before we were late.

At noontime we went home for dinner. Dad was there with Mama. He looked very sad and his eyes were all bloodshot. We sat down to dinner and he started to talk to us, but got up suddenly and dashed into his and Mama's bedroom. Mama said quietly, "Eat your dinner. Grammy has gone to live with the angels. Dad was with her when she went. You will not go to school this afternoon." Then she went into the bedroom, too.

That afternoon two of our cousins came to stay with us. We played out in the new snow and shoveled the drive with Dad. He was very quiet and worked furiously. As soon as the drive was clear, he left for Grammy's house again, while we continued playing.

The next day—Tuesday—we were all dressed in our Sunday best and in mid-afternoon went to see Grammy. Her casket was in the living room surrounded by oceans of flowers. We were led in by Aunt Edna and Mama, and we knelt on the little kneeler by the casket while Father Rivard said the rosary. It was a long kneel. Father Rivard's voice droned in a sing-song way as he repeated the prayers. He was our young priest, new to the parish. His prayers were usually as fervid as his cassock was patched. But today I noticed he was wearing a cassock without a single patch, and I thought it must be his Sunday cassock, put on especially for Grammy.

Grammy looked quite serene and even kind of pretty, although I had never thought of her as pretty before. Somehow her face seemed to have gotten more full than I remembered from the last time I had seen her. I was awed at first that she was so still, but the awe came more from the presence of the adults, who only whispered, than from any fear of Grammy. When the prayers were over, we all stood solemnly before the casket for a brief period, then we went to the dining room where great piles of sandwiches and cakes and other goodies waited to be eaten.

It was like a huge party now. People kept coming in and eating, and there was lots of kissing. Some of the women cried softly, and one or two wept hysterically. Many of Dad's aunts, whom I knew only slightly, now gathered me to their very ample bosoms, hugging me into the breathlessness of their heavily perfumed cleavages and exclaiming how much like my father I looked, while Dad beamed. I became totally confused about going to live with the angels, and didn't know whether I was supposed to be sad or glad.

The next morning was a brief replay of the previous afternoon. We met early before the casket for another round of rosary, but without food this time. Then the casket was closed and we were off to church for the funeral itself. The funeral was long and boring. Priest, curate, and altar boys hovered over the casket before the altar, waving incensors emitting aromatic fumes that caused me to go into a coughing spasm when they drifted over me. Mama was mortified and kept trying to calm me. At last the prayers and the Mass ended, and we filed out behind the casket to ride in the procession to the cemetery, where Grammy was stored away in a place that looked like a pretty neat cave.

Back at Grammy's house we ate more sandwiches and cake. I got bussed and bosomed again by all of Dad's aunts, but by this time I had learned to turn my head as it was crushed against some great aunt's heaving chest, and I came away from the encounters relatively unscathed and still able to breathe. After most of the food had been consumed, the relatives and guests departed and Dad took us home. It was early afternoon. The sun was shining brightly, and it was warm for February. The new snow had warmed to just the right wetness to make excellent snowmen and snow forts.

My siblings and our cousins spent the rest of the day building a snow fort with a wonderful defending snowman. Our friends all stopped to admire our efforts on their way home from school. Many of them joined us as we made a giant fox and goose on the front lawn. If I thought of my newly deceased grandmother at all, it was probably with some thanks that her departure from life to go live with the angels had been timed so nicely for me to enjoy the aftermath of the snowstorm in which she departed. She had admonished me indirectly to play more and not work so hard—and then had arranged for me to do just that. I am sure that as she watched us make angel wings in the snow, she was learning how to use her own angel wings, and that she, too, was pleased with the timing.

After Grammy died, Aunt Edna saw to Grampy's diet and managed the household. Grampy became more introspective and less physically active. He sold old Bob, his friend of twenty years, and gradually his garden grew smaller, he let his woodpile dwindle out of existence, and he kept only a few chickens. He was not often ill, but his life just slowed until his only activity was the job as flagman. In winter he was required to keep the crossing free of snow, a strenuous task if there had been a large storm. Dad and his brothers conspired to take over that chore, arranging for one of them to be there during snowstorms so that Grampy sat inside next to the warmth of the glowing coal stove while they shoveled. I shoveled also, stopping off from school to help. One cold, blustery February afternoon, after I had cleared the crossing of snow and lowered the gates for the afternoon mail train, I came into the little station to find Grampy wiping tears from his eyes with his blue bandanna handkerchief. I pretended not to notice as Grampy sat quietly for a bit, then said, "Franny, you very good boy for me. Make old man feel very good that you work hard for him. Pretty soon now I die. Go with Grandmamère and Grammy in heaven, I hope. You go on be good boy. Grow up and go to the college and learn big things, but always remember Grampy is very happy for you."

7

TAKING GRAMPY BACK

The year that Grammy Pelletier died, it seemed like the funeral ate up spring and summer came all of a sudden. Dad, who had been somber and tired-looking since the funeral, brightened a little and began to do the things he always did in summer, but he went about the woodpile and garden chores mechanically, with no zest. He even fell out of the habit of bringing Grampy over each Sunday to inspect the previous week's work.

One evening Dad's cousin, Nonny King, stopped by. Nonny was older than Dad, a handsome man who walked with a strange gait, throwing his left leg forward while he seemed to stand on his right, then hauling himself forward on his left leg as he wobbled on it, so that he walked in a series of lurches. I had once asked Dad why Nonny walked that way, and Dad said, "It's because of his wooden leg." Sometimes Dad had a weird sense of humor, especially if he didn't want to discuss something. I did wonder, though, what made Nonny walk that way and supposed that he had had polio, like Alice Bowles, when he was a child.

But that evening Nonny talked to Dad for a long time on the front steps. Dad looked like he was crying, but I didn't know what it was all about.

It turned out all right, though, because before Nonny left, Dad was smiling and they called me over to ask if I'd like to go on a little trip with them and Grampy. They were going to take Grampy to a place called Caucomgomac Lake, a place I'd heard Grampy talk about many times. Grampy often told me about the lake and how he used to live near there in the winter in a great logging camp. Sometimes when I was helping Grampy with his chores, he would describe life in the camp to me, carefully explaining about the things that the men did there.

Grampy told me how he went there the first time as a chopper, working hard from daylight till dark chopping down huge trees. After a few winters, though, he became a cruiser and went through the forests ahead of the crews marking out places they were to cut. I guessed cruising was better than chopping because Grampy said cruisers had their own cabin and real bunks of their own and didn't have to sleep in one big bunk with a blanket that covered twenty men at once and was loaded with fleas.

Now we were going to go there and look for Grampy's old campsites. It sounded like a fun trip, especially with Nonny along. Nonny was a friendly man who smiled a lot. He painted houses and did papering, too. Sometimes I mowed his lawn, and when I did he always paid me fifty cents.

We left on the Saturday after the Fourth of July. Dad and Nonny had spent several evenings building a huge box that fit on the baggage rack on the Model B. Nonny was a good carpenter and did most of the building. He encouraged me to help, showing me how to use the tools. The front of the box opened up into a kind of shelf that could be used for preparing food. The food was stored in the lower part of the box, while the upper part opened with another lid and held blankets and clothes. Nonny painted the box black, which made it look like part of the car. Other gear was lashed to the running board on the driver's side, and a cooler was put in back where

Paully, Nonny, and I would ride. Grampy would ride in front, while Dad drove.

Since this would be the longest trip I had ever made, Dad bought me a small notebook that said "Agrico" on the front cover and carried an advertisement for fertilizer on the back. Dad thought it would be nice if I kept a diary of the trip, recording the towns and places we stopped and anything else of interest. I was thrilled with the idea.

We left at seven o'clock. Dad always said it was necessary to "get an early start." He never went anywhere without one. It was so early that a thick layer of fog lay on the Gilman Falls Avenue flats and the several cars we passed bore down on us with their headlights on and emerged from the fog in swirls of golden mist. At the bridge the fog was so heavy we couldn't see the falls and only caught glimpses of the foamy water under the bridge.

By the time we turned north towards La Grange at the crossroads beyond the bridge, the fog had abated. By Pea Cove it was clear, and I was glad I was on the left so I could see the holy roller church when we passed it. I had been by the church many times and always hoped I'd see a holy roller rolling and writhing in the grass out in front. I supposed I would recognize a roller if I saw one, although I often wondered if they had some kind of special look about them.

All the people in Pea Cove were supposed to be holy rollers, but sometimes in passing I'd seen people by their houses and they looked quite ordinary. It was probably too early this morning to expect anyone to want to do some rolling, but I was hopeful that I might get lucky and watched carefully.

Now we were on the former Indian trail along the ancient glacial esker that had become the highway. The glacier's gravel deposit had left a ridge that ran for many miles in a generally north-south direction, standing in some places over fifty feet above the surrounding terrain. The road was like a roller coaster as it followed the varying crest of the ridge.

We wound through the town of Alton, and to our east was

Boom Birch Stream and a large bog and marsh that stretched away to the Penobscot River. It was wild land and heavily forested in places. The only farmland lay close to the road.

On Alton's west side there was a wide swath of farmland that had once abounded in rich farms, but now they were being abandoned. The early farmers had depended upon potatoes, which had done well in the rich bottomland, but potatoes are soil robbers, and without proper management the soil soon loses its fertility. The farmers had been careless, never adding fertilizers or engaging in crop rotations, and their farms soon sickened. Some turned, too late, to dairying, but the soils were too weakened to even grow good hay, so slowly the farmers gave up and turned to other means of making a livelihood. Abandoned horse-drawn farm equipment sat rusting in the fields, where alders and goldenrod were making serious inroads.

Grampy could never restrain his contempt for people who had let their farms go to such conditions. He would point out a particularly poor farm and tell us how it used to look. He blamed the decline entirely on the holy rollers, saying that the farms had prospered until the owners had been corrupted by the demon preachers who came and converted all the former Congregationalists and Baptists to holy rolling. He supported his theory by pointing out that the farms in La Grange had not suffered the same fate.

Dad made our first stop at the crossroads in La Grange village, which consisted of the IGA store that sat on the corner toward Bradburn, a garage and filling station across the road, and the post office. The IGA was an imposing structure with a set of Socony gasoline pumps in front. A tall metal pole carried a huge sign depicting a flying red horse, and a canopy extended from the store to just before the pumps.

We all got out of the Model B. Nonny had some difficulty getting out, since the car was a two-door and the front seat had to be folded down for the back-seat passengers to exit. As he got out, Nonny reached down and lifted his left leg over the seat, making his usual joke about having a wooden leg, which I still didn't think was funny.

In the store Nonny went straight to the soda pop cooler. "What will you and Paully have?" he asked. "You can have anything you want. I'm buying."

I selected my favorite, a Sunspot orange, and Paully chose a strawberry soda. Grampy had diabetes and couldn't drink soda, so he had marched over to the cooler by the counter and drank several paper cups of ice water from the jug cooler.

Nonny chose a large Moxie for himself and then spied some Frisbies over by the pastry counter, where he selected three mince. "You boys like mince Frisbies? We better get some. Going to be a while before we eat lunch." He gave us each a Frisbie and had one for himself. This was an unexpected treat. We both liked Frisbie pies.

Dad had purchased a block of ice for the cooler and several bottles of Krueger's Cream Ale for himself, along with several bottles of soda and Moxie. He arranged things in the cooler and we started off again.

It was twelve miles to Milo. The road was narrow and twisty and heavily potholed. I made my first entry in my logbook, detailing our stop at the IGA in La Grange. It wasn't very legible because of the road. There were some very good "Yes, Ma'ams" in the road and Dad made the most of them. Paully squealed with delight at each one.

In Milo, we suddenly found ourselves part of a parade. The town was celebrating Independence Day and Milo Days, and our Model B was the second car behind the parade, which was just like being part of it. Paully hung out the window and waved wildly at all the parade watchers, telling people that he was going to Caucomgomac while they stared at him blankly. Grampy sat stolidly in the front seat, gravely doffing his straw hat to any woman that waved to him and raising his right hand quite regally, as if giving a blessing to the crowd.

It took us half an hour to get through Milo. It was a hot day, and Dad was impatient to be moving to get some cool air. Nothing ruffled Grampy and he never seemed to mind the heat. Nonny, wedged in the back between Paully and me, grinned happily.

"They think you're some big shot, Uncle Joe," he kept saying to Grampy. "By golly, this is something. We come to Milo and they give us a parade right through town. Ain't this something, Uncle Joe?"

Even Dad got into a festive spirit, blowing the horn in a raucous "Aroo-rah! Aroo-rah!" and saluting with his left hand. He turned to me and reminded me to write down that we were in a parade in Milo. Then he said ruefully, "Too bad we don't have any flags on the radiator cap. That would look nice, wouldn't it? You know, one of them little sets of flags that come all together. By golly, I think when we get to Dover we should stop and buy some. We're going to be in Canada tomorrow. Be nice to show the flag."

The parade broke up just after we crossed the bridge over the Piscataquis. Dad threw the Ford into second for the long climb up Milo Hill, and we were off for Dover, rocketing along. A series of long hills made for good coasting, because the road was smooth and straight. The wind whipped our faces, cooling off the heat of Milo. Dover neared in no time at all.

Paully and I had never been this far before. Dover seemed even bigger than Old Town, but Dad said it wasn't. He detoured through the town so we could see the Blethen House and the county jail and courthouse. It was a regular sightseeing tour. We didn't stop, though, and pushed on up the road which ran along the river.

At the covered bridge to Sangerville, Dad slowed and Grampy pointed out where he had once camped on a log drive. It had been fifty years ago, but Grampy could still remember. Some kind of wood mill was on the site now, and huge piles of long logs came up close to the road on the right. I wrote it all down as fast as I could. I wanted to be sure to remember it right later on.

Guilford was much smaller than Dover-Foxcroft. There was a woolen mill right downtown by the river. All the windows were open in the mill, and we could see men and women working inside. Some were hanging out the windows and a few waved as we passed. For a few minutes it was hot again, but once we cleared the town center, Daddy picked up the speed.

The road still followed the river, dipping and rising as it did. Dad had promised that we would see the moose antlers at the Moose Horn, and we waited eagerly for them. It was a major disappointment to find only a barren pole where the moose antlers had hung for years. Dad stopped anyway, while Grampy went into the woods to pee.

A couple of boys a little older than I came by while we were waiting for Grampy and said that the moose horns had been stolen again, but there might be new ones soon, maybe even by next week. But that would be too late for us, and besides, Dad had told us that the moose horns had been there for years and years. It wouldn't be the same to see just any moose horns. We wanted to see the real ones.

It was getting past noon, and we were all hungry. Dad planned to stop for a picnic by the lake in Greenville. I hoped we'd picnic near the airplane landing site, which we did, thanks to Nonny who asked Dad to stop there.

Grampy was delighted with Greenville. He examined an old lake steamer, telling us he remembered when steamers like it plied the lakes from Greenville to Seboomook carrying passengers and towing huge rafts of logs. In the shade of the steamer, we ate the sandwiches Mama had made, washing them down with cold root beer Mama had put in the cooler and soda from the store in La Grange.

After lunch we went with Nonny to the Indian souvenir store. The store had lots of Indian souvenirs, but many were made in Japan and didn't look too much like Indian stuff. One counter bin was full of arrowheads made in Japan that sold three for a dime. The real arrowheads a little further on were a quarter each and had been made by real Indians at Kineo. Nonny bought us each a real arrowhead and three Japanese-made ones to give to our friends.

At Sanders Store Grampy bought us each an ice cream cone and gave us a quarter to buy a feathered tomahawk. I bought a red felt beanie that said "Moosehead Lake, Maine" in big letters and underneath, "Sanders Store, Greenville, Me." Paully bought an

Indian feather headdress that said "Moosehead Lake" on the head-band. We wore our new headgear as we walked back to the Ford.

Before we left Greenville, we watched several planes take off and land. One was a big warden plane with a huge cabin, a Stinson, I thought. By about half past one we were heading up the west side of the lake to the Kennebec outlet, where we stopped only briefly before pushing on towards Seboomook.

At Kineo Dad slowed so we could see Mt. Kineo out in the lake. Grampy pointed out the high cliff where the Indian maiden had jumped to her death to be with her brave, who had been killed. Grampy said it was a long time ago that it happened, but told us the ghosts of the pair still haunted the mountain.

We reached Seboomook in mid-afternoon and got a pass at Pittston Farms to go into Caucomgomac on the private road owned by the Great Northern Paper Company. Grampy got very excited as we passed by some large hayfields where men were haying, and the smell of new mown hay mingled with the scent of spruce and pine from the nearby forest. He told us how Pittston Farm used to sum-mer the horses that were used in the lumber camps in the winter. During the summer, tons and tons of hay were cut for winter feed for these horses. Horses were still being used now, but much of the hay cut at the farms now was sold, mostly to Canada.

We got to see the dam at Seboomook, which was the biggest one I'd ever seen. It had a bridge across the top which took us to the private road, a narrow, one-lane dirt road that led into the deep woods towards Caucomgomac, thirty miles away over Russell Mountain.

Shortly after we left Seboomook, I reached down to get a cold soda out of the cooler. It was close quarters, and the car was lurch-ing and bumping along at a slow speed. I had passed drinks to the others and had just removed a Moxie for myself when the Ford lurched suddenly and the Moxie in my hand struck Nonny sharply on his left shin. It should have been a painful blow, at least causing him to wince. Instead there was the dull clunk of glass on metal or wood.

Nonny never moved. I couldn't believe that he felt no pain, and I was puzzled at the sound of the blow. Without thinking, I pulled Nonny's pant leg up to reveal a strange wood and metal limb, Nonny's "wooden leg."

I was astounded. For years I'd heard about the wooden leg, but I thought it had been a joke. I looked up at Nonny and said in complete amazement, "You really do have a wooden leg! I thought that was just a joke!" For a moment Nonny looked confused, then he began to laugh. He laughed until the tears came. It had never occurred to him that I didn't know that he really had a wooden leg. Grampy and Dad joined in the laughter, too, and Paully tried giving Nonny's leg a whack with his own bottle of strawberry soda. The metal part of the leg at the calf was hollow and had large holes in it, just the size of a bottle cap. Paully discovered they made a great bottle opener, and Nonny laughed even more at this discovery.

Now we were bouncing up the steep, very rocky road to the top of Russell Mountain. We came to a clearing with the remains of a large log cabin. Dad drove off the road into the grassy clearing and stopped. Grampy nearly leaped from the car. The cabin had been one of those where he had wintered over fifty years before. He started telling Dad in French about the camp, pointing here and there and walking to various spots where the remains of the smaller buildings could be seen.

Over here was the "wangan," the place they stored food. Here was the harness shed, and over here, these low mounds with the lush grass were the remains of the manure piles behind the stables. The cookhouse still stood in trees further away. Much of the roof still remained, and inside, the stove—a giant with twelve lids and a huge oven—had settled through the rotting floor and was rusting away. The metal stovepipe was so far gone that it was only a lacy metal tube.

Paully and I investigated the large bunkhouse structure. Although part of the roof had fallen in, a good portion towards the back was still intact, although full of holes. Across the rear of the building the remains of a raised platform was still in good condition.

In places, matted hay lay over the small logs that made the floor of the platform, and there were many places where porcupines had chewed at the logs. In front of the platform a plank bench ran the length of it, making both a seat and a step up to the platform.

Grampy looked into the bunkhouse and seeing us walking about on the platform, smiled and cautioned us about jumping on the "bed." Then he explained how the men had slept all together on the platform under one huge quilt.

Outside again, we could see the remains of many campfires where others had camped, and Dad decided that we'd camp here, too, for the night. But first we would go on to the lake. The road up the mountain got even rougher and Russell Brook ran close by. The road crossed the brook in several places and the remains of old wooden bridges could be seen at these crossings, but we now forded the stream.

When we finally got to the top of Russell Mountain, the road improved greatly and we drove easily down to the lake, which we could glimpse at times through the trees. Lake Caucomgomac was long and somewhat elliptical, set in among hills. We arrived at the west end of the lake, at a clearing of several acres where there was a fine boat landing and pier, a ranger's cabin, and a float plane tied up to the pier. Next to the pier was a small, sandy beach, a perfect place to swim.

The ranger came out of his neat red cabin and examined Dad's pass. He said we could swim and added that we were welcome to camp for the night if we wished to stay. Dad said we were just going to make supper and swim before going back to the woods cabin on Russell Mountain for the night. Paully and I discovered that the water was very cold but clear, and a large school of chub seemed to have no fear of us when we swam up to them underwater. I tried to catch the chub with my hands, but they were wily and slipped through my fingers if I chanced to grab one.

While Dad and Nonny got supper ready, we swam and Grampy watched. Grampy applauded our dives off the pier, Paully's in particular, saying that Paully was a real "water dog." Grampy was a good swimmer and had been swimming with us before, but today he declined, saying that the water was too cold.

After our swim, supper was great. Dad was a good camp cook. We had potatoes and corn, thick slices of fried ham and eggs, and a plate of fresh tomatoes and cucumbers. Paully threw a piece of cucumber into the lake and it was gone in an instant as a fish rolled its back out of the water snatch it.

I had brought my fishing poles, and the surging swirl was all I needed to remind me of them. I got out one for Paully and one for me, attached a piece of cucumber, and cast my first line into the lake. I was rewarded by lunges from several directions as fish vied for the bait. My line zinged taut and my pole bent. I reeled furiously and brought in a silver chub nearly eighteen inches long. I had caught chub before, but never one more than about eight inches.

Grampy was as excited as I, and when Paully reeled in another of like size, we called to Dad and Nonny to come fish. We carefully unhooked our prizes and released them back to the lake, despite Grampy's insistence that chub up here in this cold water were very edible. He had eaten many when he worked in the camps, he said.

For the next hour we caught fish as fast as we could cast. The fish seemed to take anything—kernels of corn, small pieces of cukes, ham chunks—anything attached to the hook lured these hungry chub. The game warden came by and watched us, duly admiring especially large specimens. He said there were few visitors here, and those who came went out into the lake for the salmon, trout, and togue. No one fished for chub except to use the small ones for live bait. He admitted that he enjoyed catching them, himself.

Dad ended the fishing when he declared that we needed to start back to the woods camp. We saved two large chub, which we planned to eat for breakfast the next morning. The warden smiled and said laconically, "I've et 'em at times. They ain't bad. A little bony and muddy if the water's warm."

We got back to the logging camp with an hour of daylight left. Dad made up the beds for the night. He scraped away the hay and chaff from a section of the bunk under a section of the roof that hadn't fallen in, and before laying out our blankets, spread a thick layer of fir boughs that he cut from trees nearby. We helped with the boughs, carrying them into the cabin. Their odor overcame the mustiness of the hay and the slightly sour smell of rotting wood.

Dad made up beds for himself and Grampy, one for me and Paully, and a separate bed for Nonny. In the meantime, Grampy and Nonny had a good fire going outside and had dragged some logs up around it for seats. When the beds were made, we sat around the campfire and roasted marshmallows and ate cookies. Grampy told stories about when he had wintered here. Some were scary, all about the "loup-garou" or Canadian lynx that Grampy insisted was the fiercest animal in the world.

Grampy said that the lynx had webs between its toes, so that it had natural snowshoes and was very dangerous in winter when it got hungry. Although he had never known anyone who had been attacked by a lynx, he said all the woodsmen feared them. In very cold weather with deep snow, no man wanted to work alone in the deep woods and many would not go out at night beyond the clearing.

At half past ten Dad said it was time to turn in. Paully had already fallen asleep against Nonny's knee. The beds felt good, and we needed the blankets since it had become quite cool. I fell asleep quickly, too.

Sometime in the night I woke up. I could hear something in the cabin and was sure it was a loup-garou. It snorted and snuffled and made grunting noises just under the step to the bunk. I was really scared until I heard Dad whisper, "Be still." Then Dad's flashlight came on and an arrow of light pierced the darkness, searching out the source of the noise. The circle of light moved about the floor and picked out two pairs of eyes that glared in luminous red. There was a thump and one pair of eyes became a big porcupine as it turned to lumber away towards the door. The other followed in a shuffling gait that speeded up when Daddy threw his boot at it.

The boot woke up Grampy and Nonny, but not Paully, who slept peacefully through the porcupine raid. Dad had to get up and go get his boot, because the porcupines might come back and eat it.

They didn't return, but at daybreak some red squirrels started racing around inside the cabin and woke everyone up. The squirrels were nervy little creatures, coming quite close to check us out.

Dad got up first and started breakfast while Paully and I watched the squirrels. Nonny complained about being stiff, saying he was too old for camping. Grampy said he had slept better than he ever had when he was wintering here. He said with a big grin that he missed all the fleas—but not much.

Breakfast was good. Dad made bacon and eggs and fried the fish. They were bony but were quite sweet and not at all muddy. Nonny toasted bread on sticks for us. Everyone was hungry.

By seven o'clock we were ready to leave. Grampy walked around the clearing once more, and off we went. It took half an hour to get back to Pittston Farms, where we took the road that went to Canada. This was a single-lane dirt road like the others and very dusty. It wound through the woods past some very pretty streams and ponds, until the woods began to thin and we came out in very open country.

A sign and a narrow trail of yellow-painted trees announced the crossing into Canada, but we were still some distance from the customshouse at St. Zacharie. We arrived there about half past eight, and the customs officer was very cordial. He wanted to know where we were going and how long we would be in Canada, and asked if we were all Americans. Dad said yes, although Grampy had never been naturalized and was really a Canadian.

St. Zacharie was different from any town I had ever seen. All the houses were built right on the sidewalks and were very close together. Grampy said all Canadian villages were like that. There were very few cars but lots of horse-and-buggies with families of children all going towards the church in the center of the village.

Even their clothes looked different. Everyone seemed to be dressed in black or white. The boys and men all wore too-tight suits with all the coats buttoned up. The boys were in knickers or short pants and wore long, black stockings, the kind Dad used to make me wear but no longer did. The girls wore frilly white dresses with black stockings and flat straw hats. Most of the buggies were two-seaters with high wheels. They were crammed with children who sat quietly but waved when we drove past.

Dad stopped for gas at a McCall-Frontenac station. The pump was an old-fashioned one that the attendant operated by hand, pumping the gasoline up into a glass jug on the top of the pump where markers showed the gallons from the top down. When the hose was put into the tank, the gas ran out of the jug. We only needed seven gallons. Dad said that was because they were imperial gallons, which are bigger than American gallons. Paully was confused as to how we could put the big gallons in our small-gallon tank. We paid in American dollars and got some change in Canadian money, which Paully liked.

We stayed in Canada for about two hours before crossing back on the road to Jackman and saw more buggies and families going to church. We stopped twice while Grampy talked with some of them. The children all stood quietly while Grampy talked with their parents. He gave each child a nickel, and they smiled and said, "Merci, merci, Monsieur."

I had tried to write everything in my book, but I was running out of pages. I wished I had a camera to take pictures and vowed to buy one soon. I would have liked to spend longer in Canada, but Dad said we would get home late, as it was.

We stopped for lunch at the Bingham Dam on the Kennebec River and toured the dam, going way down deep inside. It was very exciting and scary. Nonny bought us all cold sodas and ice cream in Jackman, and we started the last leg of our trip, passing through Skowhegan and then Pittsfield. When we got home, it was nearly eight o'clock and we were tired, but it had been the most exciting trip I'd ever made.

Mama made us a big supper and listened while we told her all about the interesting places we'd seen. It seemed like the trip had taken weeks instead of just two days. I hoped that someday I'd be able to go to really far away places, because suddenly it seemed to me that I just had to see all the places that I had read about.

9

PIG TALES

Springtime is pig time for me. While others might remember past springs when the flora bloomed with special splendor and the fauna nursed new young in pasture and forest, I remember my father's annual search for the right pig (or pigs) to raise through the summer and fall for next winter's larder. For as long as I can remember, we had a pig or two in a small sty in the back corner of the garden. I suppose we could have survived a winter without the pork these animals provided, but Dad believed that his pigs were what saved us all from starvation each winter.

Ever a seasonal man, Dad followed a very strict regimen in his life that dictated what he should do in any given season. The first warm days of April seemed to start a sort of blood lust for a new shoat for summer. Almost inevitably he was disappointed when he discovered that the real spring was days away, perhaps weeks. During the time he waited, he chafed constantly. Dad wasn't a patient man. He made plans for his garden, for the potatoes and beans he would grow at Ara Brown's farm, and for the pigs and chickens we were about to get. Eventually the dandelions were in full growth on what passed for our front lawn, a sure sign that spring was finally here.

Dandelion season coincided with the fiddlehead season and, in Dad's programmed mind, the pigging season. I thought that, for Dad, dandelions, fiddleheads, and baby pigs were almost a Trinity of the Vernal Equinox.

Dad was now ready to begin his serious search for the perfect piglet. Every Sunday from early spring until late fall, Dad went for a drive on Sunday afternoons in our Model B Ford. In summer we children often went along, jammed into the back seat two deep and barely able to breathe, while Mama rode up front, jammed between Dad and Grampy Pelletier. Mama also held whichever of my siblings was the current baby—and there was always a baby.

Dad was a practical man. While he liked his Sunday drive, he did not go to view nature. All of Dad's Sunday drives had a purpose—a practical purpose. In springtime the Sunday drives were primarily designed to allow Dad to search for and find his perfect pig. While the rest of us admired the verdant landscape, Dad and Grampy conspired to drive to all the farms for thirty miles around where Dad might locate this year's prize shoat. While some of our travels were jointly enjoyable, we viewed far more farms than we did flowers, and Mama often complained that the aromas of spring were more apt to be wafting from some manure pile or pigsty than from a lovely lilac or honeysuckle bush.

Dad's idea of a perfect pig was rather nebulous. Grampy, who was the final arbiter in the purchase, preferred Chester Whites and so did Dad, but not if he could find another breed that was cheaper. Dad liked the largest piglet he could find, but he would buy a runt if the price was right. Dad did not like black or colored pigs at all. They made for funny-colored salt pork, he said. But over the years we had two coal-black pigs, a black-and-white spotted pig, a dark red Duroc-Jersey that our neighbor Charlie Miller snorted over, saying, "Whoever saw a dark red pig?" and a strange looking sow that was actually black, orange, white, and dark red. Charlie ridiculed that pig for the whole season, claiming its mother was a calico cat, much to Dad's chagrin. Of course all these creatures had one overriding qualification in their favor—Dad got them cheap.

The pigging season that I best recall was the year I obtained Maude. Maude was a memorable pig by anyone's standards. It had been a bad spring for pigging. We had made four sorties on consecutive Sundays, smelling more manure than any past season and wallowing in more stinking sties than usual. Mama was "pigged out," she said, and did something very unusual for her—she gave Dad an ultimatum. "This is the last trip. If we don't get a pig today, you go alone next week. I will not go pigging all summer."

Grampy loved my mother dearly. He looked worried and said, "I make sure Emile find good pig today, Fannie. We go for Pat Marquis farm. Pat has good pigs, him. Best pigs around on Pat's farm. And farmhouse is very pretty house, too. Dominique Marquis is fine woman, her. You and Dominique make woman talk and Emile will buy pig today for sure."

The Marquis farm was on the Olamon-Passadumkeag line, right where the Passadumkeag River emptied into the Penobscot. It was a very large dairy farm of nearly 600 acres. Pat had some eighty head of registered cows, about sixty Holsteins and twenty Guernseys producing a milk mix rich in butterfat. Pat also raised a hundred acres of seed potatoes, quantities of dry beans, and some sweet corn. He was a very successful farmer.

The farm itself was arranged postcard perfect on a triangle of rich alluvial soil, sometimes four feet deep. The barn was huge, with a Dutch-roofed hayloft that held a hundred tons of hay. Pat's house was a splendid Victorian of twelve large rooms with a gingerbread porch wrapped around the south side and west gable end. All of the buildings were painted an ochre yellow. A spacious lawn fronted the house, and Dominique had a gazebo and flowers everywhere. Mama loved to visit the Marquises, who always seemed glad to entertain unexpected guests. Mama would make one more pigging trip, just to please Grampy.

The back seat was crowded on our trip out to the Marquis farm, but recent spring floods had just receded and we children gazed in awe at the damage to the highway where washouts had occurred in several places. Costigan Elementary School was several hundred feet from its foundation and smashed beyond repair. It was Milford's last one-room schoolhouse and never did reopen. We could see the highwater marks on many of the houses in Costigan. We were all sure that Noah's flood could not have been greater.

But the Marquis house was safe and secure on the high knoll that overlooked the two rivers. I always enjoyed our visits to the Marquis farm. Dad stopped there once or twice a year, sometimes only to visit, at other times with a specific purpose in mind, such as today's visit would be. Pat always obliged Dad and Grampy with a tour of the barns and outbuildings, and in summer with a tour of a few of his choicer fields. Pat and Grampy were both Canadian-born and of the same generation, although Pat was about ten years younger than Grampy. They were old friends from years back. Pat and Grampy would talk in French, but they used English when they wanted to include me.

Today was a very warm day in the middle of May, and Pat and Dominique were sitting on the side porch glider when we drove up. They rose and came immediately to the Ford to invite us to stop for a while. Dominique—called Nicci—was a striking woman of about sixty-five with a remarkably unwrinkled face. She was taller by a head than Pat and outweighed him by at least seventy-five pounds. She favored dark blue and purple-blue dresses with very low bodices exposing the cleavage of truly magnificent breasts. Nicci was originally from the St. John's Valley in northern Maine, and she scandalized many of her Yankee neighbors in Olamon and Passadumkeag by regularly having her hair done and colored to the jet black of her youth. She dressed well, and her buxom appearance still turned the heads of many men, even those younger than she.

Pat doted on Nicci. In her presence he glowed with pride in his wife. He was of medium height and sparing in weight, being a tough, wiry man of about a hundred and fifty pounds. His face looked like it had been carved from a chunk of rock maple firewood with its high cheekbones, aquiline nose, and ice-blue eyes hidden in folds of skin from years of squinting into summer sunshine and winter snow-glare. He had enormous ears, long with full lobes, deeply cleft to his head, and a shaggy mane of iron-gray curls. At seventy-five Pat didn't look older than sixty, and his walk seemed younger, yet.

Pat and Nicci had eight children, all grown now, but several still living on the farm. The last two children had been identical twins, each weighing nearly eight pounds at birth. Both parents were proud of their offspring and their grandchildren, which were now arriving regularly. Their neighbors, all staid Yankees, were often aghast that Pat and Nicci often spoke of their children and their care in the manner that the neighbors used only for their livestock. Pat bragged exuberantly about how Nicci had nursed both twins at the same time while she knit or did some other thing. He liked to claim that their kids were like their livestock, top grade with a good pedigree.

Nicci was never fazed by Pat's admiration and broad remarks as to her qualities as a lover and mother. She smiled and accepted his praise gracefully, usually saying, "I married the finest man in the St. John's Valley. He worked hard to build this farm, and we got great kids. It don't take a big bull to be a good bull." And she would give Pat a squeeze that would nearly take him off his feet.

Today Dad asked Pat right away if he had any good baby pigs left. "I'd like at least three. One for each of my brothers and at least one for me. I like Chester Whites, which I know you raise."

Pat listened and nodded. "I got a new litter from my biggest sow six weeks ago. They ready to go now. You come see if you like." Then Pat paused and a small worried look flashed in his ice-blue eyes. "There's just one thing. That big sow got in the sty with a young black boar I got last year, and the whole litter is spotted. She had twenty-two, but she laid on five of them. But come take a look. They are all good and lively and healthy. I plan on selling about half of them. You can have your pick."

As Pat talked, we were walking to the pig sty on the back side of the barn. Like most farms in Maine with dairy cows and horses, Pat's pigsty was a lean-to built against the barn and allowed the pigs access to the cow and horse manure storage area. The pigs loved to scavenge the manure for undigested corn or oats, and it made feeding pigs pretty cheap. At the far end of the sty there was a nursery sty, a special sty with a piglet rail that kept the sow from lying against the wall and crushing her piglets. Here was an enormous sow lying contentedly on her side in deep straw while rows of black and white spotted piglets suckled side by side.

The old sow grunted occasionally, lifting her head to look at her brood, while they emitted little squeals as they slurped noisily at each nipple. Each nipple had a piglet securely attached, but there weren't enough nipples for the entire brood. A few piglets slept in a tumbled heap with milk dribbling from the corners of their mouths. They had feasted first and were the largest. They were very fit looking piglets, indeed.

There was, however, one solitary little piglet, the obvious runt, who had not fed and could not get a nipple. She raced back and forth over her siblings squealing in fury at her inability to get a nipple of her own. She was half the size of the smallest sibling, and life for her was hard. Pat grinned when he saw her. "Always got to have a runt in the litter. She's too small to be a good pig, but I keep her because she was the first one out of mama pig. She got one good drink when she was born. Ain't had a good drink from Mama since. I feed her cow milk from a bottle, but mama milk is better. But she one tough little piggy, her."

Dad and Grampy began the difficult task of choosing pigs for Uncles Ed and Ray and for Dad. Pat was asking five dollars each, which was a very fair price for such healthy piglets, but Dad wanted to be sure he got the best. Grampy was the expert on pig flesh, and he poked a pitchfork at the pile of pigs to get them up and running for better assessment. Gradually they chose three: two sows and a boar. Pat caught each of them deftly and lowered them squealing into separate burlap bags, tying the tops securely.

But Dad wasn't satisfied with his pig. The little runt had caught his eye. "How much for the runt, if I took her?" he asked Pat.

Pat sensed that Dad wanted the runt more than a little. "I tell you, Emile, I ain't sure I sell that little sow. I feed her many bottles of cow milk now. I kind of like to keep her for pet pig! See she grow up to be big mama one day. I think I have to get five dollars for her, too."

Dad took this news as though it was the joke of the century, laughing loudly and slapping his thigh. "You crazy or something? That pig ain't half as big as the others. She ain't worth more than a dollar at most. She'll probably be one of those pigs you can never get to grow pork, like those southern razorbacks. Besides, she's spotted like all the others. I got one spotted pig I don't really like. I give you a dollar for her."

Pat acted wounded to the quick. He turned to Grampy. "Joe, I know you all my life. I never know you got a dumb son like Emile. One dollar! This pig worth at least four dollars." Pat spat on the ground.

Dad ignored the backhanded insult. "Pa, I thought you said Pat Marquis was the best pig man around. Anyone can see that that pig ain't worth two dollars, but being generous because I like Pat—even if he is dumb about runts—I'll give him two dollars." Dad kicked some cow dung in Pat's direction.

Pat eyed the dung like it was plated with twenty-four-carat gold, rolling it around with his right foot. Finally he looked up at Dad and Grampy. "Joe, you are old friend. You and your Dorilda come to Nicci and my wedding more than forty year ago. But you just like that old sow there. You got a runt in your family. Emile ain't right in the head. I feel bad for you so I'm going to sell Emile this fine little runt piggy that is gonna grow up and be big mama pig for two dollars and fifty cents! I hope you tell Emile he get big bargain today!"

Grampy had been studiously noncommittal up to this point, showing no emotion whatever at the insults both men hurled. Now he grinned the big warm smile that showed off his superb white teeth and wreathed his face in happy lines. "Pat," he said, "I buy that pig for Franny here for two dollars and fifty cents on one condition. If Franny make that pig grow to be two hundred twenty-five pounds by Thanksgiving, you're going to slaughter her and other three for free when you do your own pigs."

For a moment even Pat was surprised. But he liked a challenge. To get the little five-pound piglet to that size would be a real task. He and Grampy had had many such bets over the years, and he couldn't resist this one. He took the two bills and the fifty-cent piece Grampy offered. I was elated. I had my own pig and a chance to be a hero. Dad looked like he had swallowed vinegar.

"Who is going to buy the feed for Franny's pig?" Dad questioned Grampy.

"You eat pig. You buy feed. Franny feed your pig and his pig to pay for his feed. Is very fair way to do," Grampy avowed firmly, and Dad accepted.

Pat caught the little runt and put her squealing into a grain bag, but only after wiping her carefully with another bag and giving her a last squeeze. "You be good pig for Franny," he said as she slid into the bag.

We each grabbed a bag of pig and headed for the Ford, where Dad and Pat tied them all securely to the baggage rack on the rear. The exchanges between Dad and Pat had all been part of the dickering, not to be taken seriously. Dad paid for his pigs and the pigging was over for that spring.

My brothers and sisters were enjoying lemonade and pie on the porch while Nicci and Mama visited. Pat brought out some goodies for Grampy and me and a couple of beers for him and Dad. Pat told Nicci about the arrangement with Pat over my pig, and she laughed, saying, "I hope you win, Franny. If I had been out there, I would have given you the pig. Pat just loves to sell animals so's he can dicker. You be sure and win so I see you in the fall."

We left the Marquis farm around four o'clock, almost in triumph. We had enjoyed a delightful visit with Pat and Nicci, and Dad had found his pigs. Dad was chortling in glee over his good luck in finding such prize pigs, but Mama now mumbled under her breath at the indignity of transporting four squealing pigs on a family outing. We kids couldn't wait to get home to release our piglets and admire how cute they were.

But Dad didn't stop at our house. He drove right by. "We'll

take Grampy home and deliver Uncle Eddie's and Uncle Ray's pigs. Aunt Edna is expecting us for supper, too. You can see your pigs at Grampy's house. Somewhat mollified at that promise, we stopped our complaints. Mama cheered up knowing that she wouldn't have to make supper.

We hove up to Grampy's house on South Main Street in Old Town like conquering buccaneers of old with their loot. Dad's family was already gathered, expecting us and our pigs. Dad let Mama and Grampy out, then drove the Ford to the back lot where Grampy had a pig sty. Grampy, Eddie, Ray, and Cleve all followed up the slight rise. Quickly untying the bags they released all four pigs into the sty. Uncle Ray stared in disbelief.

"They're all spotted! I thought you were going to get some Chester Whites!"

Dad was quick to respond to Uncle Ray's challenge.

"They are Chester Whites. Only they're spotted Chester Whites. They're a new breed that Pat Marquis is trying to introduce. They'll grow twice as fast as regular Chester Whites. We got 'em from Pat Marquis, and you know he always has the best."

I didn't remember Pat saying anything about my pig being a new breed or growing extra fast, but I did know Dad had a fast tongue when he needed it. Right now Uncle Ray needed persuasion that Dad hadn't been snookered.

Uncle Eddie's big moon face was wrapped in his usual jovial smile as he examined the pigs.

"What the hell, Ray. We don't eat the spots. And they're all spotted different, so this time we can tell yours from mine. A pig is a pig, for God's sake."

I pointed with pride at the runt.

"This one's mine. Grampy bought her for me to raise, and she's going to grow up to be the biggest one of all. Grampy says so."

Grampy beamed and explained his bet with Pat to his sons. Uncle Ray was delighted.

"You mean if Franny raises that runt to 225 pounds, Pat will slaughter all four for free?" Uncle Ray liked a bargain, too.

Grampy nodded. "For free for Franny. Not for you and Eddie and Emile. You boys is pay Franny regular price to kill pig. Franny pig is only one for free killing. This-a is a good way for Franny to learn to raise pigs and make money. You boys got to pay for killing pigs, anyway. Is much better you pay Franny than you pay Pat."

Dad opened his mouth to remonstrate at Grampy's plan, but Grampy put on his, "I don't listen to that" face, and Dad's mouth closed silently on his words.

Uncle Eddie chuckled. He was the oldest of the brothers and had a grand sense of humor.

"Pa, you are an old fox. But I think it's a splendid idea. I'd love to see Pat do our pigs for free, and we all want Franny here to make a buck. I think we should help him win." Turning to Dad and Uncle Ray, he added, "You guys take your pick of the pigs. I don't care which one I get."

Dad and Uncle Ray were not as generous as Uncle Eddie and flipped a coin to see who got to choose first. Uncle Ray won and chose the largest sow, of course, which also happened to have the most white. Dad dourly opted for the other sow, leaving Uncle Eddie the male. Now that everyone was happy with a pig, Dad put his pig and mine back into their bags and we went to supper.

Talk during supper was all about pigs. Past pigs, long grown and eaten were rehashed, so to speak, as their attributes were remembered. Aunt Edna, the family specialist in porcine cookery and gourmandizing, recounted tales of blood sausage-making and bacon curing. The men tended to remember the tastes of the pigs more than anything else, but there were stories about the size of certain sows, too. It dawned on me suddenly that my cute little piglet was nothing more than future sausage and possible pork chops, seriously diminishing the enjoyment of these stories for me. I had already started thinking about my pig as something other than a meal.

The evening ended early as we had to get home with our pigs. I was worried that our piglets would miss their mama on their first night away from her. I also worried about what I might feed them. Aunt Edna solved the feeding problem by giving me a quart of milk.

"This is for your pig, Franny," she said. "I want to be the first to help your pig grow big. Put some in one of Bobby's nursing bottles to feed her." Aunt Edna knew Mama had a surplus of bottles and nipples.

On the way home Dad said we would keep the piglets in a box by the stove for a few days until they got bigger and used to being alone. That delighted my brothers and sisters, who wanted to hold the pigs. Ellen, my sister, wanted to give them names.

Dad said, "You don't name pigs." He met with wails of dismay. I already had a name in mind for my pig. It was Maude, after a neighbor who was not one of my favorite people. I spoke up.

"I'm going to call my pig Maude. After Maude Martin." I could see Dad's face in the rearview mirror. I had struck a chord. He was all smiles. He didn't much care for Maude Martin after she had accused him of defecating in her spring to get even with her for not letting me tie my boat to the spring cover, which was right next to the river. I ended up having to tie my boat to a tree that was further away.

"I guess we could make an exception this year. That's a good name for a pig," Dad said. "I wish I had kept the male. I'd name it Martin. Then we'd have a Maude Martin in our pig house. But I could call my pig Martina. I guess I will." So suddenly both the pigs had names.

The next day Charlie Miller came over to pass judgment on Dad's latest pigs. Charlie talked every year about getting a pig of his own. He had lots of space for a pig sty near ours, but with Charlie it was all talk. Raising pigs requires quite a bit of time, and Charlie liked his leisure. Besides, he liked the challenge of constantly needling Dad's entrepreneurial enterprises too much, and with no pig of his own, his skills couldn't be compared to Dad's. But I noticed over the years that while Charlie came to deride, almost always he remained to praise, and he ended up taking almost as much pride in Dad's pigs as Dad did. He became a kind of surrogate pig raiser, and the two of them were very friendly adversaries.

This time Charlie eyed the two new pigs, making disparaging

remarks as usual. But when Dad told him of Grampy's little bet with Pat Marquis, Charlie became an instant co-conspirator against Pat.

"I'll have Polly save all our table scraps for your pig, Franny. Pigs always do good on fresh swill. I sure would like to see Pat have to do your pigs for free. Might even go and watch."

Maude and Martina spent a restless night. They missed their mama and only stopped squealing and rooting around after Mama filled the hot water bottle with piping hot water, wrapped it in an old towel, and put it in their box. They curled around it and finally went to sleep.

In the morning I fed Maude her first bottle of milk in her new home. She stood on her hind legs and slurped noisily, pulling with surprising strength on the nipple. Martina got fed a mixture of milk and chicken mash out of a dish in her box. She enjoyed it and gobbled it all down. My brother Paul was a little perturbed that she got chicken mash and worried that she might grow feathers or something.

That evening Dad and I tightened up the pig house and the pen so that our little pigs couldn't get out between the boards, then we put in clean new hay Dad got from the Stones' farm. Maude and Martina raced around the pen squealing and rooting up little furrows in the soft soil as we worked. Charlie was as good as his word and came over with a small pot of Polly's leftovers from their supper, which Dad accepted after commenting that they really looked too good to feed to the pigs. Polly was a great cook. We watched as the pigs attacked the food with great gusto. Martina kept snarling at Maude, trying to hog the food for herself. But alone with Martina, Maude fared far better than she had in the litter. She was nimble and could avoid Martina's jabs, at the same time snuffling up mouthfuls of food from under Martina's snout with great dexterity. I was greatly relieved to see this. I had worried that Maude wouldn't stand a chance against the bigger pig.

In two weeks Maude doubled in size. She didn't catch up to Martina, but she was growing faster and it was easy to see that she was trying. I scratched her back and belly several times a day with a small stick and she got to be a contented pig quickly. She knew me and responded to my voice and the food I brought her. The bottle got to be a problem, though.

I was feeding her skim milk that Dad got from the Stones for free. All their cows had freshened and they had a surplus. Harry Stone dropped off about five gallons a day in a clean five-gallon jug. The milk was fresh and sweet, newly milked the night before. Although it was supposed to go to the pigs, we kids drank as much of it as the pigs did. It was the first time we had all the milk we could drink, and we drank a lot.

Maude loved the milk, too, but the bottle was a problem because she sucked so hard she kept pulling the nipples off. Dad showed me how to wire them on and make the holes bigger. Now the problem was that a baby bottle of milk wasn't enough and she needed several refills, which was a nuisance. I solved that by using a quart soda bottle as a nurser. It was tiring work and I felt like a wet nurse, so I devised a holder for it which worked well. After drinking her fill, Maude flopped over onto her side and gazed imploringly at me, waiting for a good scratch on her belly. She was rapidly becoming a spoiled foster pig-child.

Maude and Martina enjoyed the surplus milk for over a month and grew with amazing speed. By late June, Maude had caught up to Martina in length but looked kind of slab-sided. Dad was convinced she was going to be a razorback, but Grampy declared on his weekly Sunday visit that she was going to be a prize if we gave her time. I think he was trying to reassure me.

Maude also had Charlie's support, for he had taken a liking to her, too. Every evening when he brought his daily ration of leftovers for Maude's feeding trough, he lingered to scratch her. Maude loved the pampering, willingly throwing herself down to submit to Charlie's scratching stick. Maude was a happy pig.

By now our family garden was also growing well. The green pea crop would be ready for the Fourth of July, which was always Dad's goal with peas. Maine families took Independence Day seriously in those days. It was my favorite holiday, since I loved the fireworks and the thrill of shooting off firecrackers. Flags flew all over town. There was a parade in the morning with all the veterans and American Legionnaires arrayed in their military best with flags waving and some properly patriotic speeches delivered. The men spent the afternoon shooting off the more powerful firecrackers, to the entertainment of all. It was a patriotic time in a far less sophisticated world than we know now.

Most families dined on fresh garden peas, tiny new potatoes dug prematurely from the family patch for the occasion, and fresh Atlantic salmon from the waters of Penobscot Bay. The potatoes and salmon were slathered in egg gravy. There were cold and dewy watermelons, strawberry shortcake, and lots of drinks for everyone. A washtub full of iced beer and soft drinks graced every back yard.

We'd been nursing our pea crop along with careful weeding, throwing all the weeds we pulled into the pigs' pen. Our garden was a large one, over half an acre. Charlie Miller had a garden, too, about half the size of ours, all generating enough succulent weeds to half fill the small pen.

Maude, especially, seemed to relish burying her wet snout in the freshly pulled weeds, tossing her head to throw the weeds into the air to cascade over her back. She would root through the weeds, picking out all the chickweed first, eating it roots, dirt, and all with a greedy glint in her piggy eyes and her curly wisp of a tail flicking in mad circles. As pigs go and being sister pigs, Maude and Martina were quite mannerly when eating. Oh, a little shove here with a snout wasn't uncommon, or a little flip there with a hip to get some special morsel, but they dined quite formally for pigs. Not so when they discovered pea shells.

Mama cooked for our growing family on a grand scale, restaurant style. Her normal pot of green peas came from a bushel of shells, which got dumped into the pig pen. One whiff of those fresh pea shells, and Maude and Martina went into a feeding frenzy. Maude, slightly smaller still than Martina, couldn't compete with her stronger sister and got rudely shunted aside at first. But Maude soon outwitted Martina. While Martina, with her head high, blissfully chewed and savored the sweetness of a mouthful of pea shells, Maude shuffled around her, carefully rooting a heap of shells into a corner two feet away. She left Martina a few tidbits, enough to divert attention from the hoard that Maude had accumulated. Then Maude stood with her budding hams braced against any bunting or shoving and munched on the peas she had corralled in the corner.

That Fourth of July I dumped a full basket of shells in the pen, deliberately putting most of them in Maude's corner. Maude didn't even look for a scratch when there were pea shells. She did what pigs do best—eat. The fireworks going on didn't seem to frighten the pigs at all. I even threw several OK Salutes into the corner of the pen, but after the first bang, the pigs didn't startle.

Our Fourth of July party took a turn no one expected when I later went back near the pigpen to get some more tin cans to blow up with firecrackers. The garbage can was behind the shed, which was separated from the pigpens by Dad's pea patch. As I leaned into the trash barrel to retrieve an empty can, I heard a grunt and felt a wet something nuzzle under my short pants. I straightened, turned, and was greeted by a leering Maude.

I couldn't believe what I was seeing. How did she get out of our escape-proof sty? At least Dad had said it was escape proof, and he always built everything with overkill. But Maude was out. She stood straddle-legged just out of my reach, her snout and flanks covered in the rich loam of Dad's pea patch and several long strands of vines dangling from her maw. Vines? Vines! Oh God! Not vines! I lifted my eyes over her back and scanned the pea patch.

No Man's Land at Chateau Thierry never looked as bad after the German shelling. In the middle of the desolation stood Martina in a total mud pack, calmly chomping on the remains of Dad's pea crop—the prolific Telephone variety, for which he was famous all over town. The look on Martina's face was pure porcine pea passion. While I watched she delicately plucked a long pod full of peas and munched, clearly savoring each mouthful.

Maude, meanwhile, eyed me suspiciously, then backed into the patch, put down her snout, and proceeded to plow a furrow through the only standing peas left. I was horrified. I had to sound the alarm. But to do so would be to court disaster, because I knew who was going to get blamed for the escape—me. No matter that Dad had designed and built the pen, declaring it pig proof. I did the feeding, and I had been admonished a thousand times to check the pen to see that the pigs hadn't rooted under it. I hadn't checked in more than a week.

I made a diving leap for Maude, just four feet away. I touched pig hide, but only barely. With a loud squeal she slipped out of my hands with lightning speed and dashed off a good ten feet. Then she stopped and glared back at me over her shoulder, as if to say, "Don't ever touch me unless I ask. When I want a scratch, you'll know." I knew then that I needed help and started back to the party.

Everyone was facing the street, watching Dad and Charlie prepare a charge in Charlie's cannon. I edged up to Mama, who was holding Bobby, our latest sibling, figuring I'd tell her and she could relay the message. Dad wouldn't kill her. As I tapped her on the shoulder, I felt the cold, wet snout of another exploratory goose.

Mama started to say something to me—which became a scream as she lifted Bobby to safety high over her head.

"The pigs are out!" Mama shouted, as I turned, dreading what I might see. Maude was a safe four feet back now, trailing a snoutful of prize vines that wound gracefully around her forequarters. Several yards back stood Martina, similarly draped. The cannon went off with a thundering roar, which was immediately eclipsed by a roar twice as loud from Dad.

"How in hell did those Jeezly pigs get out?!" There was a sudden pause and complete silence. Dad seldom cussed, so everyone was doubly awed over the cussing and the escape. Another roar issued from Dad.

"My peas! Those friggin' pigs have been in my peas. We have to catch them before they go back and damage the patch."

I thought, "If you only knew," but didn't say a word.

Dad and Charlie came barreling up the lawn, each going for a pig and clearly expecting to grab her and hustle her off to the sty.

Charlie made the first lunge. Martina squealed like—well, like a stuck pig—and made a bouncing jump to the left. Charlie bit the dust in a slide that would have done Babe Ruth proud.

Dad, on the other hand, was somewhat more familiar with pigs than Charlie was. He elected to use ruses and wiles.

"Nice girl, Maude. Good piggy. I'm going to give you a nice scratch." He inched his way to just beyond arm's length and made the grab. A sudden dive, a wild squeal, a violent oath, and a cloud of dust as Maude deftly eluded capture a second time.

Dad and Charlie called for a parley to discuss strategy. Dad had a bright idea.

"We have to get something to feed them so we can get close to them. Franny, go pull up some of the pea vines that have been picked over. That will fetch them."

My luck just ran out. "There aren't any," I said.

"What do you mean there aren't any? There must be two thousand square feet of peas out back of the shed. Go get some." Dad didn't take being contradicted so easily.

"Well, there were a lot of peas out there, but I think the pigs must have been loose for awhile. It's mostly all rooted up now. And I think they ate most of the peas." My voice faltered with the news.

Dad had a tendency to pop his eyes when he was excited or angry. His eyes popped like the blisters on your heels from a new pair of shoes. Forgetting all about the pigs, he dashed to the shed and disappeared momentarily. Everyone expected another roar, but Dad reappeared looking as if he'd been pole-axed between the eyes. He shuffled up to Mama like a zombie in a B movie and said in the saddest voice I ever heard, "They ate every pea, Fanny. Every pea. They didn't leave us any."

Mama loved green peas, too, but she usually did most of the shelling, besides the cooking, and it was hard to tell whether she was sad or glad. But she handled it well.

"That's too bad, Emile. I know how you love them. We'll just buy whatever you need from Harry Stone. But now we have to get the pigs back in the pen."

Her comment brought Dad's attention back to the pigs, which he seemed to have forgotten momentarily. Both pigs were staying just out of reach of anyone who tried to get near enough to catch one. There was a lot of discussion going on about the best way to catch a pig. Vernon Johnson insisted that we get pails to pull over the pigs' heads. The idea sounded preposterous to me, but strangely enough Charlie and Dad decided to try it. Dad ordered me to get a couple of five-gallon paint pails from the garage, which I did.

The strategy was for one of the women to approach the pig from the front, offering a tidbit, while Dad and Charlie sneaked up from behind and clapped a pail over its head. No one planned any further than that.

Charlie's wife Polly offered Maude an enticing half a hotdog in a roll. Maude trotted up to sniff the delicacy oblivious to Charlie tiptoeing up behind her. When she'd almost reached the hotdog, Charlie sprang forward with poised pail. Vernon shouted, "Swing it down now, Charlie," and Charlie tried to get the pail over Maude's head.

He never had a chance. Maude spun around in a flash and fled between Charlie's legs, sending him in one direction and his five-gallon pail in another. Polly dropped the hotdog as she toppled over backward. Maude, unwilling to give up the tidbit, turned back and in a lightning dash ran lengthwise over Charlie, snatched up the hot-dog, and retired ten feet away to gulp it down—just as Dad made his stab at bucketing Martina.

Martina, although bigger, didn't have Maude's vitality or speed, and Dad actually got his bucket over her head. She squealed and kicked, but Dad hung in there, and finally Martina stopped backing and stood quietly, head in pail.

Dad was triumphant. He had bested Charlie and captured Martina. He yelled, "Someone grab her before she gets loose again. Grab her by the hind legs."

No one was too anxious to do that, but Vernon decided he knew pigs and now was the time to prove it. Vernon was a big young man, a lineman at the University of Maine and a College of Agriculture major. He grabbed Martina around her middle and lifted her off the ground. She must have weighed about thirty-five pounds, every pound squealing, kicking, writhing pig.

With Martina in his arms, Vernon started for the pigpen. An entire gallery of watchers formed an entourage to guide and counsel him on the trip. I ran ahead, and at the fence I plugged up the sizable hole the pigs had rooted out under the lower boards, just as Vernon lifted Martina high enough to throw her over the fence. Martina had calmed somewhat, but it wasn't over. When Vernon had her hind legs clear of the top board of the fence, Martina unloaded her final surprise. The pig poop ran down Vernon's chest in a big smelly blob just before Vernon dropped her into the pen. Vernon was the hero of the moment, but no one offered to shake his hand.

It took another hour before we caught Maude, finally trapping her in the shed. All the really young children had been herded into the house to keep them from hearing the increasing vulgarities of the desperate pig posse, and for a while it was a tossup over whether we would have the usual nighttime fireworks. A hiatus was declared after Maude's capture, so the captors could go home and clean up, then we had the fireworks. They were an anticlimax after the pigs.

Maude and Martina proved impossible to keep penned. For the remainder of the summer they got out every other week or so to raid and savage. Charlie's cucumber patch succumbed to them, and the Johnsons' flower beds. They didn't become docile until mid-September, by which time they were well over a hundred pounds each.

Maude got to be longer than Martina by late October, but I worried that she didn't seem as fat. We started her on whole corn and cooked potatoes, and she finally started to gain fat. By mid-November I was sure I had a winner. Grampy beamed each Sunday as he beheld her, but I began to feel bad and it got worse as the time neared for slaughter in December.

The second Saturday in December was the execution date. I had told Grampy I didn't want to eat Maude. He tried to explain that pigs are food, not pets, but he didn't change my mind. I could see that it worried him that I was feeling bad, so I did my best to look sad when he came by with Pat Marquis to make the final arrangements.

Pat took one look at Maude and conceded the bet. In fact, he was ecstatic over her, climbing into the pen and running his hands all over her.

"This one fine pig, her," he said. "This pig is show pig for sure, but she is crossbreed. Too bad for that." And he shook his head sadly. Then his face brightened.

"I tell you what, Franny. I like to have Maude for brood sow. I buy her back from you for fifty dollars, Emile. What you say? She be very happy mama pig on my farm for long time. Okay?"

Fifty dollars for a pig! Dad couldn't say no to that and didn't. I had the financial summer of my life with the money I got from Uncle Eddie and Uncle Ray for slaughtering their pigs. I didn't charge Dad for Martina, and he practically glowed with pride when he looked at all the money I had made, forgetting all the pig chasing he'd done.

Maude had grown to two hundred and sixty pounds, outweighing her siblings by over thirty pounds. So Maude was saved, and we ate Martina. She had the best pork chops I'd ever tasted, but we had to nail them to our plates to keep them from escaping our forks.

9

THE DERAILMENT

Out by the railroad tracks behind the Millers' barn, there was a very small pond. Its source of water was a small swamp across the tracks which fed the pond through a culvert under the roadbed. The pond sometimes got very low but never went completely dry.

In the winter there was usually enough water to make a very small skating rink with only a little work. Sometimes a hummock of grass that had grown too profusely in the summer had to be cropped, or the bulrushes trampled down, but Tommy and I didn't mind those tasks, often making a game of it by attacking the rushes with hand saws swung like machetes. We would pretend we were hacking our way through the jungles of Panama, preparing the way for General Goethals to push the canal through the fierce jungle growth.

I had read an account of the Panama Canal construction in an old *National Geographic* magazine in my Grampy Spruce's attic and had told Tommy about it. At first Tommy was skeptical of the account, thinking I had imagined the whole story, but then he had to concede to its truthfulness when I showed him the magazine article. I never returned the *Geographic* to its place in the files since it also had a story about the Bantu Nation of South Africa and had some fine photos of the Bantu women in full native dress. The women wore mostly strings of beads around their hips and bangles on their arms. While Tommy found the account of the canal's construction interesting, he found the account of life in Bantu Land fascinating, especially the pictures of the native women. I kept the magazine stored in our woodshed, stuck in between the tiers of firewood. Tommy liked to borrow it for overnight. If he wasn't cooperating about something, I used the magazine as a bribe and he usually capitulated.

In springtime the pond behind the Millers' barn would swell, and we could float a raft on it that we'd constructed from old railroad ties left nearby by the section crew. The old ties of Eastern cedar floated quite well, despite their years of service to the railroad. Held together by spruce slabs from the summer slab wood supply in my yard, they made a fine raft that served in many capacities. It was a pirate ship on some trips, undertaking raids on the Spanish Main, sinking Spanish galleons, and carrying us as captain and crew on a murderous, careening journey to the Caribbean islands of old.

In early spring, when the pond teemed with small frogs and salamanders, we mounted expeditions to capture these wild and ferocious animals. At those times the pond and marsh became deepest Africa, and I became Frank Buck capturing man-eating crocodiles from the depths of Lake Tanganyika at risk of life and limb. Or Tommy would stand in the tall rushes with an extended hand, saying, "Ah! Dr. Livingstone, I presume," in a veddy, veddy English accent.

Our raft also served as both the *Maine* in Havana Harbor and the *Lusitania* off the coast of Ireland. If there was still sufficient water to float the raft at Fourth of July, an hour on the *Maine* was a sure bet. We'd pole to the middle of the pond and then throw OK Salutes at the Millers' barn, which had become Morro Castle overnight. The

Salutes were pretty powerful, and after several of the barnboards had been blown away, Charlie Miller took a dim view of our game.

I even devised a way to blow up the raft itself in a reenactment of the original sinking. If the OK Salutes were coated with wax, they would sustain immersion for a limited time and I could wedge a number of them in the cracks between the ties, leaving only the fuses out of the water. These were lit and we jumped into the murky water before the explosions. Great geysers of water shot into the air while we stood in the muck and shouted, "Remember the *Maine*" with great patriotic fervor.

A similar scenario was played out for the *Lusitania,* this time with skulking U-boats waiting to send forth torpedoes. There was much shouting of, "Torpedo in the forward hold, Sir. Torpedo amidships, Sir. She's listing hard to port. Away all boats! Women and children into the lifeboats first!" I could be very nautical if the occasion called for it, and Tommy likewise.

We also liked to play on the railroad right of way, although it probably wasn't a very safe place to play. There were five trains a day during daylight hours, plus the shifter that came up two or three times a week from Bangor to move boxcars on the siding. We knew when the trains were due and stayed clear of the tracks at those times. We got to know the sectionmen, and when work parties were in the area we would tag along, watching the men. The sectionmen were all local people with families and boys of their own. They were good-natured men, sharing goodies from their lunch pails with us, joking, and telling stories on each other for our entertainment. No one ever told us to stay off the right of way.

Sometimes we liked to place soda bottle caps on the tracks before a train was due to pass. When the train ran over the caps flattening them, we used them as play money. The colored caps from different types of soda would have different values, from pennies to silver dollars.

Our success with this encouraged further experimentation, and I discovered that when I placed an eight-penny nail on the track, a freight train would turn it into a nicely flattened, dagger-like knife. It only took a little filing to sharpen the edges, but it proved difficult to attach a proper handle. We decided to try larger nails and early one morning placed sixteen-penny nails on the track, some on each rail. We were planning to make several large knife blades for daggers or stilettos. We knew that the mid-morning freight train went through at 10:30, and we planned to come back then to retrieve our blades. But we miscalculated on one factor.

I had forgotten about Lewis Longtree, the section chief track inspector. Lewis made a daily inspection of all track from the Greenbush siding to the Penobscot River Bridge. He did this inspection on his handcar, an Irish Mail-like vehicle operated with a set of handlebars that were pulled forward and backward to supply power to the gears and wheels. It worked quite easily once underway.

Lewis lived on his farm at just about the mid-point of his territory. The tracks passed through his farm, cutting his pasture in half, and the railroad had erected a small shed where he stored the handcar when it was not in use. Lewis put his handcar on the tracks each day, usually sticking to a regular schedule. One day he would go south to the bridge in the morning and north to the Greenbush siding in the afternoon. The next day he would reverse the schedule. When he reached the depot in Milford each day, he would go to Spruce's Store for whatever needs he might have. He would also pick up his mail at the back of the store. Lewis liked to time his arrival for noon or 5:00 P.M. to ensure that there were other men picking up their mail; he could learn what was happening in town and add his input into any of the affairs that he felt might require such.

On the day that we loaded the tracks with sixteen-penny nails, Lewis made his morning trip. From the semaphore at Glasgow's Hill it was a long downgrade all the way to the depot. Lewis could crest the grade at the semaphore, head south, and then practically coast to the depot three-quarters of a mile further on. On this particular morning Lewis was early, since he had business at the Old Town Depot. He crested the grade and pumped vigorously, so that he was soon flying down the tracks at a good speed.

By the time he reached the "W" sign a hundred feet before the frog pond, Lewis was rocketing along at twenty miles an hour. The "W" sign was to warn southbound engineers to blow the whistle for the grade crossing a quarter mile ahead. Lewis later said that it should have meant "Whoa," because just as he passed the sign, he saw the nails on the track.

It was much, much too late. Handcars do not have very effective brakes. Lewis did his best, but he hit those nails hard. They bunched under the wheels and as the handcar rode over them, it derailed. It careened off the tracks and went flying along the embankment before sailing out into the pond in a magnificent spray of water. The handcar came to rest in the very center of the pond, sinking into thirty inches of muck and blue-green algae. Lewis's lunch bucket, an oval one with a tin cup that fitted upside-down on the lid, flew off the carrier rack behind the saddle, to land several feet beyond the handcar. The impact caused its cover to fly off, and although the bucket landed upright, it quickly turned turtle and sank, carrying Lewis's lunch to the bottom of the pond.

Lewis was unhurt. He sat astride his wayward handcar in stunned disbelief. In his thirty years on the railroad nothing like this had ever happened to him or to anyone he knew. His striped overalls and denim shirt were covered in green slime. His engineer's cap dangled from a cattail. Once he got his breath back, he roared a string of invectives and curses that were heard in the nearby houses.

My mother heard them and rushed out to bring the little ones inside. Charlie Miller, on summer vacation, heard the curses. Sam Hesseltine, in his shop sharpening saws, heard the outburst. Sam and Charlie arrived on the scene just as Lewis was slogging his way through the slime to the roadbed.

Charlie Miller always liked a good joke, and now he couldn't resist a chance to get a crack at Lewis.

"That's one hell of a place to take a bath, Lew. If I knew you wanted one that bad, I'd have invited you in to use mine. What the hell do you think you're doing, anyhow?"

Lewis, busy trying to scrape off the slime and muck and shaking water out of his overalls and boots, was near apoplexy. His rage was enormous. He kicked at the nails scattered along the tracks, knowing full well how they had come there.

"I'll skin the kids alive who put those nails on my railroad," he vowed. "I'll see they don't sit good for a month, damned kids!" He mouthed more obscenities.

Sam Hesseltine stood by in quiet awe. Sam was a skinny old man with a big Adam's apple that bobbed up and down when he spoke. When Lewis finally quieted down a little, his wrath spent in the futility of kicking the rail and the nails, Sam said, "By golly, Lew, I seen you go by here pretty speedy sometimes, but you must have been going like the hammers of hell today. 'Nother eight feet you'd have made the other side and never wet a whisker. Just warn't your day, I guess."

Charlie chuckled, "Well, maybe 'tis Lew's lucky day. He ain't hurt none. Just his pride is a little scratched at. Lew, you ain't got no broken bones or nothin', have you? You can't have. You've been making too much noise to be hurt at all. Me and Sam will help you get your handcar out of the muck and you can come over by my garage and I'll hose you down good. We'll get the slime and stink of this muckhole off you, and you'll be all set as soon as you dry off."

Getting the handcar out of the muck turned into a strenuous chore. It took an hour of tugging and pulling and the use of Sam's block and tackle before the deed was done. The work proceeded with much cursing on Lew's part and considerable needling on Charlie's. Charlie was all the time thinking about what a great story this was going to make at noon mailtime at the post office. This event could be a topic of conversation for at least a week, and he'd see that Lew remembered it for even longer.

By the time the handcar was clear of the muck and safe by the tracks, all three men were mired in slime and mud. It was very warm, so at Charlie's invitation they all retired to the picnic spot by Charlie's garage to hose down. Word had spread about the accident, and children had gathered to watch the retrieval of the machine and now the baths, standing in wide-eyed wonderment at three grown men bathing in their clothes in the middle of the day on Charlie's lawn.

Tommy and I were off swimming at the river all this time and knew nothing about what had happened. When we remembered our nails, it was well past the time when the freight went through, and by the time we arrived back at the pond, Lewis had put his handcar back on the track with Charlie's help and had gone on to the Old Town station.

Tommy and I were picking up the nails scattered along the rails, wondering why they were unflattened, when I looked up to find Charlie staring down at me. Charlie had a half smile on his face and a real chuckle in his eyes as he asked, "What you fellas doin'?"

I knew he had plainly seen what we were doing and I couldn't lie about it, but I needed time to figure out just why he was taking so much interest in our activities. I sensed that Charlie knew about the nails, though, so I said as innocently as I could, "We were going to play in the culvert but we saw these big nails and decided to pick them up to use in the camp we're building over in the woods."

Charlie was aware of our camp. He had contributed used lumber, old nails, some windows, and other parts to it. He looked down at me steadily.

"You boys still building that camp, eh? You're lucky to find these nails. They look like new. I wonder how they got out here by the railroad track. Seems like a funny place to find nails."

I glanced over at Tommy. His face was white and his eyes wide. We both knew something was up. I desperately played for time, hoping for some clue from Charlie.

"Probably fell off the section crew's motorcar," I replied to Charlie's musing. "The section crew was putting in new ties just the other day. We saw 'em, didn't we, Tommy?" My lie was brilliant. The section crew was always working on the tracks somewhere.

From long habit, Tommy knew exactly what to say.

"I seen boxes of nails and lumber on the motorcar when they was here. They must have lost quite a few nails. Good thing we found 'em."

Charlie's face assumed a serious expression and he nodded his head.

"You're right. Too bad you boys didn't find 'em sooner. See them wheel tracks all over the gravel there?" Charlie turned and pointed, and we saw the tracks in question. A dread fear took hold of us. Charlie went on.

"Seems like Lew Longtree come down grade a while ago, going like a bat out of hell as usual, and he hit some nails on the track. Wound up out there in the middle of the pond. Him and his handcar. Now, by jeebers, he's some mad. I 'spect we better not tell anyone about how careless his section hands are with his nails. No tellin' what he might do. Probably fire the lot of 'em, and I guess that would be too bad. I won't say anything if you fellas don't. Maybe you fellas ought to check out the tracks more often and make sure no more nails ever get on 'em."

Tommy and I fell over each other in agreeing to Charlie's suggestions, assuring him we'd look for nails diligently, and if we found any, we'd remove them from the tracks—for sure.

Charlie made sure he got to the post office before the noon mail came in, though. He was seated real cozy in his chair by the stove—which, of course, didn't have a fire in the summer—waiting for Lewis to come in for his mail.

Lewis came in right on schedule. His striped overalls were a little strange looking, wrinkled like they had just come out of the clothes basket, un-ironed. When Lew spotted Charlie sitting there like a coldhearted preying shark that has caught the scent of blood in the water, he knew he was in for it. By now his anger had cooled some and he had begun to see the humor of his flying leap into the frog pond. He decided that his best bet was to let Charlie have his fun and take his ribbing with as much grace as he could. Lewis nodded to Charlie as he passed his chair, went to his box, and got his mail. It was then that Charlie asked, "How you feelin', Lew?"

There were six or eight of the usual men there. They all sat up at once at that question. They sensed immediately that Charlie was up to something—that he had something on Lew that he was dying to let out. It was the phrasing that was the tip-off. Charlie had asked way too much. If he had simply said, "Nice day, Lew," or "This is a warm one," no one would have taken notice, but to be so loquacious meant something. They waited to see what it was.

Lew wasn't going to make it easy for Charlie. "Not too bad, even though I had a bad morning."

"That so," Charlie replied, with a surprised and questioning look. "You looked like you was having it pretty easy there this morning when you was taking a bath in the frog pond back of my place. Do you do that often?"

Lew maintained his composure even though he wanted to take a swing at Charlie that would have knocked him into the middle of next week.

"No, I can't say I do. But this morning I got up feeling sleepy-tired. Couldn't get awake somehow. All the way down from my place I felt plumb tired. After I passed Glasgow's, I was worse. I was sailing right along, too, 'til I came to the whistle sign and seen that pond. That's when I decided to wake myself up for good and all. By gawd, I took a flying jump right into the middle of her. Me and my hand-car. Woke me up real good, 'cept the water was a little too warm for me. A dite on the murky side, too. That's why I was sittin' out there in the middle when you come by. Seems kind of a silly thing to do now, but at the time it seemed like a good idea."

All ears listened raptly as Lew recited his version of the morning events, and although Charlie had lost most of his edge with Lew's recitation, he slapped his knees and laughed while he described what he'd seen.

"Damnedest thing I ever see," Charlie chuckled. "I was washing my car and I see Lew coming down grade. Next thing I knew he was sailing through the air like an aeroplane. His hat blew off and he disappeared into the biggest splash of water and green slime ever come out of any swamp. I figured for sure he'd been killed deader than a doorknob and run over to see. There he was, sittin' on his machine turnin' the air blue with his cussin'. He was some perturbed. I'd give a ten-dollar bill to see him do it again!"

Amidst the laughter and further queries, Lew exclaimed that it would take more than ten dollars for him to repeat the performance, and allowed that it was something that—now that it was over—he'd just as soon have missed.

Knowing the true reason for Lew's bath, Tommy and I were loathe to meet him for some time, fearing that he may have found us out. We were playing pirates later that fall when we saw Lew coming down the grade. This time he stopped carefully. The pond was very high from fall rains, but the water was clear. We were on our raft in the middle of the pond. We thought we were in for it at last but Lew merely strode along the roadbed, surveying the pond. Waving to us, he said cheerily, "Don't fall in, boys. That's one hell of a place to take a bath." Then he got back on his handcar and went on to the depot.

10

CRANBERRYING

Cranberrying was part of the ritual of life in Milford. In winter families cut cordwood, going to woodlots each Saturday to cut until enough cords were accumulated. In spring the cordwood was sawn to stove length and stacked to dry for winter use. Late spring was garden time, and early summer was for strawberries and blueberries. Each season had its chores. Cranberries were for August.

Cranberries grew in abundance on the Sunkhaze Meadow. They were free for the picking, and my father and uncles harvested berries for our families every August. It wasn't easy. Cranberries are perverse in their growing habits. They grow in very wet marshes and peat bogs, hidden low in the tall marsh grass and sedge. The berries grow most abundantly on the undersides of the bearing bush, where it is difficult to see them and almost impossible to pick them by hand. We harvested them with a specially designed rake that was pulled through the low bushes by hand. It was backbreaking work, but the berries were worth it. These small, sour berries would grace the tables of many townspeople on Thanksgiving Day and Christmas, but for others they were a daily staple for as long as the supply lasted into the winter months.

I went cranberrying for the first time when I was nine and was included each year thereafter as part of the annual rite. I went with mixed feelings. I loved being included in that elite group of my father and his brothers Ed and Ray and the other pickers on the marsh, but the day was long and often very hot. My task was to carry bags for the berries and put up the streamer-topped alder poles that marked the location of the filled bags in the vast expanse of the marsh.

The flags were necessary because the tall marsh grass concealed anything left in it. It grew to six or seven feet in height, with wide, saw-toothed blades that could inflict shallow but wicked cuts on one's face or hands. Walking in the grass was extremely difficult, since it grew out of an underlayer of sedges and peat that stayed wet even in the driest years. Walking across the marsh was like wading through a very wet, soft sponge while being beaten with a grass broom.

Sunday was the day chosen to go to the marsh. I would go to early mass with my father and uncles, and then prepare for the day's outing. The store's Model A pickup was packed with bags, rakes, lunches, and water jugs, a canoe was strapped atop the load, and we would drive the four miles to Sunrise Farm. If the summer was dry, it was possible to drive directly to Sunrise Landing on the bank of the stream; otherwise it was a mile walk with gear and canoe.

We launched the canoe at the landing. Uncle Ray, who had never learned to swim and hated the water, was first into the canoe. He was placed in the middle on the bottom, and all the gear was loaded around and sometimes over him. Uncle Ed took the stern paddle. He was a huge man, almost 300 pounds, and a powerful paddler. Dad sat on the bow with me just behind to balance the craft. The canoe was a 20-foot Old Town and capable of carrying a large load.

The run from Sunrise Landing to the picking areas was about a mile or so. As Sunkhaze Stream meanders through the eleven miles of meadow, it is from 20 to 40 feet wide and very deep, 8 to 12 feet on average. The stream bed is a tortuous one, winding and twisting its way like a liquid snake through the meadow. The best cranberries were to be found near the area known as the "oxbow," because of two very sharp S-curves that found the stream paralleling itself for a quarter mile. Many canoes had come to grief in the oxbow because the breezes around the curves were hard to judge. Canoeists paddling in a dead calm, mirror-like stream could round a sharp S-bend to find a stiff breeze whipping up sizable waves that could capsize a heavily loaded canoe.

Uncle Ray was not unaware of this danger and feared it. For some unknown reason, it never occurred to anyone to provide Uncle Ray with a lifejacket. He took his chances, but not without a steady monologue of directions and admonishments to his brothers. Uncle Ed, in particular, found Uncle Ray's discomfort funny and offered him the reassurance that were they to capsize there was no need to worry about drowning, since the leeches would bleed Uncle Ray to death before he could drown.

When we got to the cranberry area, we were faced with disembarking. Back at Sunrise Landing there had been a semblance of a beach where the canoe could be drawn out of the water, but here the canoe could only be pulled up alongside the water's edge, which was deep. While Uncle Ray held the canoe against the bank by clinging tenaciously to clumps of grass, the canoe was unloaded of its cargo. Then he scrambled out into the grass himself. The men could now get on with the harvesting of the cranberries.

There was no shade at all on the meadow. A few alder clumps were scattered here and there and an occasional small willow, but none grew much taller than the grass itself. The tall meadow grass obstructed what breeze there was, and by mid-day the meadow was extremely hot. Any breeze seared the skin rather than cooled it.

By noontime perhaps seventy-five people were on the meadow, all working diligently in the searing heat to gather the berries. After an hour or so of raking, everyone felt some discomfort. All suffered from grass cuts, were thirsty, or felt the effects of the grass pollen blowing in the breeze. It was monotonous, tedious work.

But the monotony didn't seem to dampen the spirits of the cranberry pickers. As their paths crossed, they would pause to talk and exchange gossip and jokes. There was much laughter and good-humored conversation.

The meadow abounded in deer, which remained hidden in the tall grass, resting quietly in the sun unless a picker came across one while searching for berries. When this happened the deer would bound to its feet in great panic and go leaping off to a more secure spot. As the panic-stricken deer leapt one way and then another, men and women popped up out of the grass, waving their arms and shouting to turn the deer from its escape.

Regular pickers at the meadow were Ned Ouillette and his wife, an oddly matched pair known in Milford as "river people." They lived in a small house close to the river near Barker's Mill and sustained themselves by picking berries, fiddleheads, and dandelion greens in season and by making craft goods such as Indian baskets. Ned was a first-rate carpenter, also, and was often hired for his carpentry skills. They were a true Jack Sprat couple—Ned was as thin as a reed and his wife was tall and extremely fat. They had no automobile but owned a rowboat that Ned had built. They used this boat to go everywhere on the Penobscot and its nearby tributaries, and had rowed twelve miles up the Penobscot and Sunkhaze to go cranberrying. They often made trips of several days' duration.

Although Mrs. Ned—as she was known—was enormous, she was fairly agile and seemed to walk about in the spongy meadow with no effort. Inordinately powerful for a woman, she could carry a seventy-five-pound bag of cranberries with ease, heaving it across her broad shoulders and trudging with it to their boat more easily than her husband seemed to.

Mrs. Ned raked expertly and with fervor, gathering as many berries each day as any man on the meadow. She was one of the few women in the area who ventured onto the meadow, most of them objecting to the total lack of sanitary facilities or even a good clump of bushes to provide a modicum of privacy. Mrs. Ned was nonplused. When she felt the need, she simply lumbered away from the general crowd to find a secluded place to squat in the privacy of the tall meadow grass.

One day when Mrs. Ned was off in the grass, someone startled a deer, which kept bounding about trying to elude the berry pickers who popped up at every turn. There was much waving and shouting, with everyone participating. The terrified deer finally escaped its tormentors and bounded off in great, floating leaps in the very direction that Mrs. Ned had recently taken. It made a desperate leap, soaring through the air in a long, graceful arc, to come to earth atop Mrs. Ned, who was squatting in the grass in supposed security.

It's hard to know who was the most surprised—the deer, Mrs. Ned, or the other pickers. While Mrs. Ned rose from the grass screaming some very earthy epithets, the dazed deer regained its feet and loped off over the meadow. Mrs. Ned emerged from the tall grass in regal wrath at the indignities she had suffered and stalked back towards the main group of bystanders.

Their good-humored catcalls and remarks soon restored her usual cheerful nature. The description of the event in the *Penobscot Times* the following Thursday turned out to be a source of great personal satisfaction for her, since Mrs. Ned had never before had any claim to fame. The clipping decorated a cabinet door in her kitchen for many years.

Unlike the Ouillettes, who picked cranberries in order to sell them, most of the pickers picked berries simply because they were hooked on cranberries. My father and uncles could have picked all the berries they and their families needed in an hour, yet they toiled hour after hour in the broiling sun and stifling humidity to pick until every bag was full.

When the last bag was full, they would load the canoe with the day's harvest. If the trip upstream to the meadow had been a little dicey, the trip back had to be downright dangerous. With Uncle Ray seated mid-canoe on the bottom, gear and berries stacked around him, the canoe was loaded until only two inches of freeboard remained. I scrunched on my knees behind my father in the bow, cautioned to sit still at all costs.

Off we went. With great exertion, my father and Uncle Ed

could get the heavy canoe moving. They weren't overly skilled canoeists, but they were careful and proceeded slowly, making turns carefully and paddling in rhythm. Their efforts were constantly monitored by Uncle Ray, who alternately pleaded to be let out to walk, or cursed their ineptitude. On each trip we would inevitably ship a little water, and Uncle Ray's wails of fear would ring out across the meadow. Dad and Uncle Ed would jeer at him, while Uncle Ray vowed to the Virgin Mary that he would never again come on such a lunatic excursion.

After we'd landed and unloaded, everyone seemed to forget the discomforts and miseries of the day. We were exuberant about our harvest, primed for the "great giveaway." Like pirates of old, we were returning to our lairs laden with booty, which we would now bestow with great largesse to all our friends and relatives. Usually we ended up with just enough berries for our own Thanksgiving and Christmas dinners.

I used to wonder why we went to such great efforts over cranberries. Some of the pickers wouldn't have eaten a cranberry on a bet. But after all the work and the heat and the insect bites, I liked to go with Dad while he distributed the berries, and enjoyed the talk and the laughter and the grateful thanks we received. I decided that it wasn't the berries that was important, but rather the adventure. When we returned from the meadow, we returned like heroes. And everyone likes to be a hero, if only for a day.

11

THE PERFECT TREES

Christmas was a very special time for our family. It was exciting to think about the presents we'd get from our aunts and uncles and from Santa. As I grew older, I learned that Santa was a euphemism for Mama and Dad, a fact that I struggled to accept at first, but then resigned myself to with great reluctance.

While the Fourth of July was an exciting day of unbridled exuberance and patriotism, fantastic fireworks, and noisy cama-raderie with all the dads and boys of the neighborhood, Christmas was more personal, more intimate. I looked forward to opening pre-sents with my aunts and uncles and grandparents all sitting around and beaming and smiling at my pleasure.

But I wasn't selfish about Christmas. I shared it with Paul and Ellen and Anna and the others as they came along. I was as pleased as Ellen was over her dolls and Anna over her teddy bears. Of course, I thought they were pretty girlish and silly, but I was happy that my sisters got gifts they wanted and liked.

I got trucks, and one year I got a zeppelin that became the

envy of all the boys in the neighborhood. The only problem with the zeppelin was that Junior Eastwood kept taking it home with him and then screamed when I tried to get it back. Junior was pretty rough on toys, and each time he took it home, the zeppelin came back with another dent or scratch.

I liked the toys, the sleds, and the bobsled I got one year—they were wonderful gifts that lasted for years. Ned Ouillette had made the bobsleds that Paul and I got. Mine was bright orange and Paul's was red. We enjoyed them immensely despite some jeering remarks from friends who had sleds built by Mr. Glasgow, who was considered to be the master builder of bobsleds in town.

But by third grade I was asking for books, lots of books. Mitts and bats were fine, but they were things. Books—they had stories of adventure! They contained descriptions of people and places. They transported me into other worlds, other lives, acquainting me with heroes of earlier times in strange lands. Books contained facts and fantasies in endless abundance, if one could only read them all.

I'd started with the *Bobbsey Twins* in second grade, moving on to other series after finishing *Honeybunch, The Five Little Peppers*, and others of that age group. Then I discovered *Aesop's Fables* and the fairy tales of Hans Christian Andersen and the Brothers Grimm. They enthralled me, and I went into a near trance-like state as I immersed myself in the stories.

It wasn't just the stories that delighted me. The new words were thrilling. That one could use so many different words to describe and depict scenes, events, people's thoughts—anything one could imagine—was a source of wonderment. New words, words not used in everyday conversation, abounded in books. Sometimes a particular word I'd never encountered before would take such hold in my mind that I would have to try it out.

At first I tried them out on Tommy, but Tommy often scoffed at them, so I learned to try them on Mama. Mama liked to read, also, and was quite understanding about not making sarcastic comments on my more daring choices of words. She did get a strange look on her face one day when I was recounting a lively conversation with

Tommy and said that "Tommy ejaculated." I'd come across the word in a *Tom Swift* book and thought it had a nice, rolling lilt to it. Mama asked if I knew the meaning of the word.

"Oh yes," I said. "It means to squirt out, like when you squeeze toothpaste from a tube." Mama smiled, and it wasn't until a few years later that I learned why she'd asked.

So Christmas was a time when I looked forward to replenishing my reading stock. Strangely, while few of my relatives were as avid readers as I was, they all contributed to my stock of books, often giving me several in addition to other presents. My Aunt Enid and Aunt Pearl were particularly generous in that respect, as was Uncle Wilfrid, my mother's brother, who was also a prodigious reader.

All of this Christmas giving made me want to give gifts in return, but I needed to find some means of earning money so that I could buy gifts for all my relatives. Money was a scarce commodity in our house. Grammy Spruce would give me a nickel or a dime once in a while, but I seldom saw much money otherwise. Uncle Wilfrid had given me a subscription to *American Boy* magazine, and its monthly arrival just reminded me that I needed to give gifts, too.

By fifth grade I was earning twenty-five cents a week filling the wood box for Grampy Spruce every day, but that would hardly suffice. Christmas was approaching. Miss Weeks, the fifth-grade teacher, had asked for volunteers to cut a tree for the fifth- and sixth-grade room. I had been chosen, and felt it was a great honor. I was determined to bring in the tallest, fullest tree the entire school had ever seen. I had a week to find such a tree, and I knew that I would.

I began looking the next afternoon, after school. Across the railroad tracks in back of our house was a tract of land of a thousand or more acres belonging to the Jordan Lumber and Land Company. It was primarily pulpwood country, an ideal place to find the tree. I cut through the woods to the tote trail halfway to the Call Road and trudged its length, scanning the treetops for a suitable tree. I found none. I retraced my steps, this time scanning the smaller trees in the undergrowth. They were all miserable, puny trees, suitable only for Tommy's house. Tommy always seemed to pick a tree with hardly any limbs, a trunk slightly larger than a match stick, and limbs so thin that a single ornament caused them to sag in agony from the weight.

It was starting to get dark, and I still hadn't seen a single tree that measured up to my standards. I returned to the fork where the trail diverged toward the Call Road. On impulse I went left at the fork, instead of going home. I'd only been that far out once before, and the woods were strange to me. I hurried along in the fast growing darkness, hoping to loop back to the road before complete darkness settled over the woods. My spirits were low. I'd expected to find a tree quickly and was now worried that I wouldn't find one at all.

The trail bent to the right and the woods thinned, allowing the remaining daylight to brighten the trail considerably. Suddenly, off to my right, I spied a kind of open glade. It was quite bright, and the little remaining light revealed Christmas trees of every size, in abundance beyond my wildest imaginings.

I hurried closer and found that beautiful, thick trees grew everywhere, each one nearly perfect, with short, thick trunks growing close to the ground. These trees were lush and thickly green and smelled deliciously of balsam even in the cold, late afternoon air. I'd found the mother lode of Christmas trees, a nirvana of nature where nothing but perfect trees grew. Each tree seemed better than the last. I couldn't decide which to cut. It was now too dark to make a good choice, so I decided to come back the next day, when I could pick the very best one. My only concern was remembering just where the glade was. Back at the trail, I hacked a blaze into a large hemlock. The clean white wood stood out starkly against the blackness. I could see it even in the dark.

As I started for home, it came to me like a revelation that those trees were especially placed there for me to find, and that they would allow me to fulfill my wish to give presents to all my relatives. I could cut and sell those trees to people in town.

At home, my usual before-supper radio programs—"Little Orphan Annie," "Tom Mix," "The Ralston Straight Shooters," and even "Bobby Benson and the H-Bar-O Ranchers" failed to keep my mind from my secret. I had vowed to myself that I'd tell no one about those wonderful trees. They were mine. I had discovered them, and I just knew that I'd been meant to.

I returned to the glade the next afternoon. In the full sun, it was even more spectacular than I had remembered. Now I traced a pattern through the trees until there before me stood The Tree. It was taller by far than any of the others, a full ten feet, I was sure. It was thick! So thick that the trunk could only be glimpsed. It was perfectly shaped, tapering from six feet in diameter to a perfect top spindle of ten or more inches. I circled it several times, admiring its perfection and envisioning it festooned in Christmas decorations in our classroom, aglow with colored lights. It would surely be remembered in years to come as the most glorious tree ever to grace Miss Weeks's classroom.

It seemed almost a shame to cut such a beautiful specimen, but it had to be done. I cut the trunk quickly with my axe and saw, and the tree fell with a majestic whoosh, a sound befitting its grandeur. I trimmed the stump close to the ground, then trimmed the base of the tree to a precise squareness, ready for a stand. Slinging my saw over my shoulder, with my axe in one hand, I grasped the lower limbs to drag the tree home.

A sharp tug barely moved my prize. To my dismay I found I could scarcely budge the tree. Exerting every muscle, every sinew of my body, I finally got it going, but it was tiring work dragging the tree, and after a quarter of a mile I knew I couldn't go any further. Pulling the tree off the trail, I hid it in a thicket of fir and decided to get Tommy to help. The tree was now far enough from the glade so that Tommy would think I had cut it nearby.

Tommy had just gotten home from his father's store, and when I explained my dilemma, he readily agreed to help bring the tree in. We returned to the woods, pulled the tree from the thicket, and attached a short rope we'd brought with us. The rope made it easier to drag the tree and several inches of crusty snow helped, but it was still tough going.

It was long after dark when we reached my house. We were both hot and tired, but not too tired to call Mama and all the kids to come out and admire the tree, which we'd stood against the garage. All agreed it was a tree of beauty.

Tommy showed up to help again the next morning, along with Paul and Albert Eastwood. They hoisted the tree onto their shoulders and staggered with it to the top of the hill, where Dalton and Chester Buck joined our ranks. By the time we reached the school, there was no room for further help, and I'd ended up acting as parade marshal, guiding the entourage up the steps and into the school.

Miss Weeks had been forewarned of the imminent arrival, and although she was usually very much in command and always a little formal, she seemed caught up in the excitement. Even Mr. Bolling had dropped his facade of aloof command and was very genial and complimentary. The spirit of Christmas had been dragged into the school along with the tree.

There was an alcove in the classroom where the tree was always placed. This tree graced the same spot as previous trees, but it was different. It filled the alcove, its height reaching within inches of the ceiling. The branches swept out in a regal manner, seeming to embrace those who came near it. The children could hardly wait for Shirley MacCallum to come and put a stand on it.

Before the day ended, the tree had been given a stand and each grade had been allowed a class period to decorate it. Of course, the other grade couldn't be stopped from watching, so there was little formal learning that day. Miss Weeks held an hour-long Christmas carol session after the tree was decorated.

Christmas trees for the other two rooms had also arrived that day, but they were poor comparisons to my tree. I went home feeling like a hero, and the feeling lasted until Christmas recess. Even the Christmas gifts at school seemed better that year. The ten-cent limit on expenditures was adhered to very scrupulously, yet everyone received nice little gifts, and there were no gag gifts. My Uncle Ray always provided ice cream cups, and this year the ice cream was augmented by cookies from Tommy's father's store. The real store-bought cookies brought smiles of pleasure from all the children.

After delivering the school tree, I returned to the glade every afternoon to cut another tree or two. These were all smaller trees, suitable for home use. I went about town from door-to-door peddling the trees, which I priced from twenty-five cents to a dollar. They sold readily. In fact, I found it difficult to keep up with the demand. The money was rolling in.

I'd mentioned my enterprise to my parents, and they commended my industry but asked no questions. I sold my last tree on the morning of the day before Christmas. I had fourteen dollars, a fortune. I asked my brothers and sisters what they'd like for gifts, and I consulted with Mama for helpful suggestions for my aunts and uncles. She suggested that lacy handkerchiefs were nice for the aunts, and red or blue bandanna handkerchiefs were wonderful for the men, or better yet, a real linen Sunday-best handkerchief.

I took careful note after reassuring Mama that I had the cash. This surprised her until I showed her my treasured earnings. Then Mama was truly impressed with my diligence and business acumen.

That afternoon I went on a shopping spree at Woolworth's and Grant's in Old Town. I bought eight sturdy water glasses for Mama. They had flowers painted on them and cost fifteen cents each. I bought Dad a new pocketknife with two blades and a complete tool kit besides. I bought little toys for each of my brothers and sisters. I bought each of my grandfathers a necktie for a quarter each. The ties were very Christmassy and had a tag on the back that said "cravat" in red embroidery, which I thought was a true mark of excellence.

I really outdid myself on my grandmothers' gifts. I found gift-boxed antimacassar sets for a sofa for fifty cents each at Woolworth's. Each set had one large doily for the center of the sofa and matching smaller doilies for each side. I thought they were beautiful. The boxes were decorated with red poinsettias. Mama's suggestions for handkerchiefs proved a grand idea. I was able to find boxed sets for everyone well within my budget. I went home having spent slightly more than half my money. I'd save what was left just in case I didn't get the pair of hockey skates I wanted for Christmas.

At home Mama helped me wrap all the gifts, exclaiming over the fine choices I'd made. I was careful to keep Mama's gift hidden from her and wrapped it last. The packages were done up mostly in red or green tissue with lots of seals to hold the wrapping in place. They looked good, even if they were a little lumpy.

This was a memorable Christmas—the first when I'd been able to give gifts from money I'd earned myself. My aunts and uncles were profuse in admiring their presents, saying the handkerchiefs were just what they wanted and needed. Both grandfathers wore their new ties on Christmas Day to church, afterwards showing all who would look the embroidered "cravat" that I'd pointed out to them. My grandmothers adorned their sofas with the new antimacassars, cautioning the family to be careful of them and not to soil them.

Mama used her new water glasses for Christmas dinner, and Dad made a great show of throwing away his old pocketknife with the almost-worn-out blade, now that he had a shiny new knife loaded with tools. The younger children loved the new toys I'd bought: Paul the whirly sparkler machine and Ellen the celluloid doll that looked like a Campbell Kid. I got my hockey skates, along with over twenty new books, which included a complete set of *Airplane Boys*. I'd never enjoyed such a wonderful two weeks.

By the following May, the memories had dimmed, but not disappeared, when one Sunday Uncle Ed, who was a deputy sheriff of Penobscot County, came to visit in the afternoon. While Mama talked with Aunt Flora, I sat with Dad and Uncle Ed. I was reading one of my Christmas books and only half listening to Dad talking with his brother. That soon changed.

"You know, Emile," Uncle Ed said, "I had the damnedest case to look into about a month ago. Frank Davis out on the Call Road called me to report a robbery. Seems like he had a grove of Christmas trees he'd been growing in the woods back of his house. Nursed and pruned those trees for nearly five years, he said. Said he was going to harvest them come next Christmas. Well, sir, he went out to give them another spring pruning and there weren't more than a dozen left—and only the scrawny ones at that. Those trees had just disappeared during the winter sometime. We searched the area and never found a clue as to how or when they went, but by jeebers, they're gone!"

My heart was pounding. The room grew hot. A vision of that wonderful little glade with the beautiful Christmas trees stood before me in such clarity that I was sure both Uncle Ed and Dad could see it, too. All the trees danced before me. The superb tree that had graced my classroom led the parade with Miss Weeks and all the children ringed about and singing in joy. The other trees joined in the dance along with the people who had purchased them. And they were all so joyous and happy. But the most joyous of all were Frank Davis and his wife, who had purchased a tree for a whole dollar and had been so pleased when I delivered it that Frank had given me an extra fifty cents. And for his own tree!

Dad's voice finally dispersed the vision, scattering the trees and people as he said, "Probably some kid trying to make a buck got 'em, or some of those Call Road Copes got 'em. They are a rascally bunch, you know."

Uncle Ed sighed, "That's the way I figured, but wouldn't you have thought someone would have seen one of those trees being cut? Whoever got 'em must have been as smart as a whip. Well, I suppose we will never know." And closed the subject.

12

A Suit for Lawrence

The Eastwoods were a large family who lived four houses down the street from us. There were four boys and two girls, most of whom were older than me. They lived in one of the Jordan Lumber Company houses—the one closest to the old mill yard, across the highway from the Upper Mill Lumberyard. It was a good place for a family to live because there were lots of places for children to play.

If you counted all the space at the lumberyards—which the Eastwood kids considered their territory by right of living in a Jordan house—they had ten acres of space in which to play. This included the favorite summer swimming place on the river, just three hundred feet from their front door. The river had a big eddy in front of the Eastwood house and was an ideal place to skate in the winter. The steep bank, rising a hundred feet to the Congregational Church at the top of the hill was perfect for sledding and skiing.

Because they were the largest family and lived closest to these areas, the Eastwood children became the resident caretakers. The rest of us acknowledged their assumed rights and deferred to the Eastwood children in matters of where the diving board would be placed, where the ski jumps would be built, and where the bobsled runs would develop. Living as they did within the bounds of Milford's favorite playgrounds, the Eastwood children were the first to defile the virgin snows of winter with their bobsleds and skis, the first to lay out ice rinks on the newly frozen Penobscot, and always the first to plunge into the still-icy river when the spring floods had passed and the waters had become a quiet backwater eddy.

The four boys of the family—Howard, Lawrence, Albert, and Charles—were clones of their father, Charles, Senior. Charley Eastwood was a tall man in his late forties when I first met him. His six-foot-plus frame was lank, but the muscles of his limbs were steely. Charley was nearly bald and had the beginnings of a paunch that was slung low under his belt. It made him look pregnant, especially in the summer when he worked in his sleeveless white undershirt. Everyone liked Charley. He was an amiable man of no great intellect, but he received the ultimate compliment in town when people stated emphatically, "Charley Eastwood is a worker." That accolade was enough to ensure his status in town.

Howard, a youth of sixteen, looked much like his father, but while Charley tended to be talkative and gregarious and showed some intelligence, Howard was phlegmatic, reclusive, and dull. He rarely smiled and seemed to have been born aged. He was big for his age and very strong, but his strength was like that of an ox—useless unless directed and guided by some intellect other than his own. No one could tell if Howard was happy—his face lacked expression.

Albert was a year younger than me, and dull like Howard, but happy. A smile always played on Albert's face. Albert liked everyone. He fawned on people as a puppy does, ready to throw himself on the ground belly-up for a friendly scratch. Albert's cocoon of love was so thick that no insult ever penetrated it. He was too big to suffer any physical insults. Punches and physical assaults on his person never fazed him. He was proud of his toughness and often encouraged his friends to hit him. When they did, he never blinked but delighted in the attention.

Lawrence was the different one in the family. Everyone agreed that Lawrence was smart. A few said Lawrence was brilliant. Another few said Lawrence was a genuine genius. And there were a few people in town who said that Lawrence couldn't be an Eastwood at all. His father, Charley, worked shift work at the Bangor Hydro-Electric Company powerhouse, and a few insinuated that Charley's wife wasn't always lonely on those weeks when Charley worked the midnight-to-eight shift. But Lawrence bore a resemblance to his siblings and to his father, even though he looked smart and they didn't.

I liked and admired Lawrence, who was two years older than me. Lawrence liked to read and read everything he could get his hands on. He had no books of his own. None of the Eastwood children had any toys except some sleds and wagons that Charley had made for them. Except for their homemade toys, the Eastwoods depended on the toys of other children for their play. When I was six, Mama gave me a birthday party and invited Lawrence, Albert, and Charley, Junior. They all came with a present for me. Junior presented me with a wind-up toy truck which he let me unwrap, but then he took it home with him when the party was over. He also kept taking the zeppelin that I'd received at Christmas.

Lawrence borrowed all of my books, but he was meticulous in always returning them promptly and in good condition. He seemed to remember everything he read and was always hatching schemes to put his wealth of knowledge to work. He had a vivid imagination and an active brain.

Charley was a handyman and had a host of tools, which he let Lawrence use. Lawrence soon became as skilled at making wagons, sleds, toy trucks, and gadgets as Charley was. It was Lawrence who erected the first diving board at the swimming hole in front of his house. I was enlisted to help. Lawrence stole the planks from Barkers Mill. I stole the nails from Dad's garage. The diving board was a huge success from the first day. It was well engineered, too, being made of three two-inch-thick clear spruce planks, each one shorter than the other and laminated into a single unit like an auto spring.

The diving board projected over the river at a spot in the ledges where there was ten feet of water at the shore which quickly went to nearly twenty feet. It stuck out from between two small elm trees, ten feet above the water. Lawrence wrapped burlap sacks around the planks, offering good traction when a diver ran out on them. There was lots of spring provided by a pair of coils that had once been part of an Oldsmobile. Lawrence "found" the springs at John Davis's garage and saved John the trouble of having to dicker with the monthly junk dealer over their worth. As people observed, Lawrence was smart.

Lawrence and his cousin James liked to build model airplanes of balsa wood and they introduced me to the art. Lawrence was very good at making models and patiently showed me how to cut the parts and apply the glue. None of my planes flew very well, but Lawrence's always did.

Once Lawrence made six World War I biplanes—two French Spads, a Fokker Tri-plane and a Fokker DVII, and two British Camels. He invited a group of boys to the Old Mill Lumberyard where he staged an exciting dogfight for us. All six planes zipped into the air at once, their rubberband-powered propellers whirring. One Fokker, one Spad, and one Camel each carried a one-inch fire-cracker that had been lit just before the plane was released. The resulting explosions blew the models to smithereens in a most satis-factory recreation of the shooting down of the *Red Baron.*

Blowing up models that cost twenty-five cents to buy was expensive, but Lawrence was resourceful. He began to invite other boys to watch—but they couldn't watch for free. A fee of ten cents was charged to all spectators. Lawrence enlisted Albert's and Junior's help in collecting the fees and flying the models, but while they did very well launching the planes, they failed to collect many dimes. Albert couldn't bear to turn away anyone without a dime, and Junior refused to give Lawrence the dimes he collected, so Lawrence got his sister Leona to handle the gate.

Leona proved to be an inspiration. She was fourteen and old enough to command respect from the younger children, but her most valuable asset was her looks. Although she had long, lovely auburn hair, it was wasted on her. She was covered in freckles, and her face was small and pinched, with close-set myopic eyes behind thick glasses. When she asked for the ticket money, the boys were glad to pay just to get her to go away. From then on Lawrence's dog-fights thrived financially.

It was about this time, when I was building a model of the famous Waco Crop Duster with Lawrence, that Lawrence told me how he was saving his money to buy himself a suit of clothes for graduation from eighth grade, an event Lawrence looked forward to with great optimism. He was getting the best grades in his class and expected to be the class valedictorian. He often saw me in my suit going to church on Sunday and said he wanted one just like it. My suit was a double-breasted brown pinstripe flannel with two pairs of pants—one long and one knickers. It flattered me that Lawrence envied my suit, especially because I wasn't too happy about wearing the knickers and preferred the long trousers.

Lawrence asked if I knew how much a suit cost, and we discussed the price of a complete wardrobe of suit, shirt, shoes, and tie. We concluded that Lawrence would need nearly twenty dollars to outfit himself in the manner he desired. Lawrence had asked his father if he would buy him the suit if he was the valedictorian. The lure of scholastic honor wasn't anything Charley had ever aspired to himself, but he did agree to pay half of whatever such a suit might cost. Lawrence had been trying to save for his suit ever since, but money was scarce.

Despite the fact that Lawrence seemed to have money for models and the others always had money for candy at the store, the family was poor. They never seemed to wear anything but rags, and in winter the children often played outside even on the coldest days without mittens and in thin coats and jackets. The boys had cracked and bleeding knuckles. They didn't seem to mind the cold, although Junior would sometimes sit in the snow and kick and scream in a tantrum because his feet were cold. Albert would look at him with his smiling face and say, "Junior's cold. Crying warms him up." It seemed to do that, too, because he never went home and would stop if no one paid attention to him.

Sometimes when I was at the Eastwoods' with Albert or

Lawrence, their mother would offer me a biscuit and jelly. They never had bread. The biscuits were bitter and heavy, and they used cheap oleo that hadn't been colored. They never had milk. Isetta, their mother, could make excellent cakes, however, and I was always glad to eat her chocolate cake even if I didn't care much for her biscuits.

Isetta made lots of stews and soups. Much of their food was grown on the little farm the family owned in Greenbush. They spent several days a week there in the summer, traveling back and forth from Milford in the truck Charley had made from a 1929 Chevrolet sedan. They kept pigs and beef cattle there, too. But all this bounty still ended up as soup or stew. I often wondered if they had more than one cooking pot.

Their house was almost devoid of furniture. The kitchen contained a table and chairs for all. The dining room/living room also had a table and chairs, a battered couch, and one rocking chair for Charley. The four bedrooms on the second floor contained only a bed and dresser, no chairs, no curtains. There were no pictures on the walls or decorations of any kind. There were no rugs or linoleums on the floors, and the bare floors were unpainted. But the house was spotlessly clean. Isetta, her oldest daughter Bertha, and Leona scrubbed the place endlessly. The only amenity was a small radio by a curtainless window in the living room. Yet the family seemed happy.

In the fall when I was in sixth grade, Lawrence took sick at school one afternoon. He was often sick, and was thin with very poor skin color. Although he was strong for his size and a good athlete, he seemed plagued with stomach troubles. Lawrence often stayed home for a day or a half day with an upset stomach or diarrhea, so no one thought much of his latest illness. He was home for a day or two, then the stomach upset abated and he was back in school.

Several times this occurred. It was just before Thanksgiving that a very severe attack of indigestion struck Lawrence. His parents treated him with the usual home remedies, a laxative and aspirin. Lawrence didn't respond to treatment and grew worse. He became feverish and there was some swelling in his groin. After a day or two the pain ceased, but his fever grew worse and he became almost comatose. Charley and Isetta decided that the services of a doctor would have to be obtained, money or not. Doctor Madden was called.

The doctor arrived just before suppertime and found Lawrence pale and feverish, very weak, lying on the battered couch. Doctor Madden was renowned for his skill and his bluntness.

"What did you bother calling me for?" he bellowed. "Couldn't you idiots see that this boy has something more serious than a belly-ache? He's got appendicitis, and it's a cinch the appendix has ruptured. I'm going to try to save him, but I fear I'm too late." The doctor was clearly distressed at his inability to stave off what he knew was inevitable, and it enraged him.

Lawrence was carried to Madden's waiting Ford and they raced off to Eastern Maine General Hospital in Bangor. The doctor was so enraged and furious that he even got his Ford into high gear, a gear he rarely used, preferring to roar along in a grinding second gear. Madden was a skilled surgeon, one of the best in Eastern Maine, but his skills were no match for the raging peritonitis caused by the ruptured appendix. Lawrence died that night, shortly after the operation, his thin body ravaged by the germs it could not fight.

The sad news spread quickly in the neighborhood as neighbors went door to door. The next morning, as Tommy and I walked past the Eastwood home, Albert and Junior were outside. They came to the sidewalk to talk. Albert was his usual smiling and uncompre-hending self.

"Lawrence died last night in the Bangor Hospital. He had germs in his stomach. We ain't going to school today at all."

Junior was also unperturbed by his brother's death. "Yeah, we don't have to go to school. Mama says we're going to have a funer-al for Lawrence on Friday and he'll get lots of flowers. They're going to bring Lawrence home in a casket tonight so people can come see how he looks. Are you guys gonna come see Lawrence?"

I'd been to see my grandmother when she died, but she was

old. Lots of old people died all the time, but I'd never heard of a boy dying, especially a boy I'd talked with and liked. The idea of going to see Lawrence dead was scary and sad. I remembered how Lawrence had been saving money for a suit for graduation, and now there wouldn't be any graduation for Lawrence. I really wished Lawrence hadn't died like that, without even telling anyone. Of course, Lawrence probably hadn't planned on dying just yet. I had never thought about being dead myself until just then. Neither Tommy nor I answered Junior's query.

As we walked on to school, we talked about Lawrence. We agreed we would miss him, but neither of us felt like crying. We just felt saddened that we wouldn't see any more of his dogfights or inventions and toys. He really didn't seem dead, even though both Albert and Junior seemed to know he was.

School was somber that day. Miss Weeks announced that Lawrence was "deceased." It was a word I didn't like. It meant dead, I knew, but somehow it was like saying Lawrence was more than dead, that he had been erased, like he had never been here at all. Dead seemed better. Deceased people were strangers in the newspaper, not people you knew.

That afternoon after school I saw the big wreath of flowers on the front door at the Eastwoods'. Albert and Junior weren't outside, but Isetta came out and told us we could come back to see Lawrence. Isetta's eyes were red and her face blotchy. She said she knew Lawrence would want his friends to say good-bye. We were invited for Friday noontime with all the schoolchildren. Both of us promised to come, and Isetta went back into the house after giving each of us a big hug. That made me feel sad, but not for Lawrence. I felt sad for Isetta.

Mama and Dad were sad, too. They didn't say much, but I could tell they were sad. They seemed to look at me and my brothers and sisters differently, as though someone was waiting to snatch each of us away. Dad and Mama got dressed up nice and went down to the Eastwoods' for two hours "to be with Charley and Isetta," Mama said. When they came back about nine o'clock, Mama had been crying, too. And I was sad for Mama, just like I'd been for Isetta.

On Friday morning our teachers told all the classes that they would be dismissed at eleven o'clock and all those who wished could go to see Lawrence. It was a very cold day, and the five-minute walk to the Eastwoods' house left everyone with red cheeks and runny noses. There was a line of children waiting at the kitchen door. Charley came out and he had a suit on. That surprised me, because Lawrence had told me that Charley had never owned a suit. Charley had all of us come into the house, although it filled the house jamb-packed-full.

Lawrence's casket was in the living room by the window that looked out over the swimming hole. The children went up in groups of four to gaze on Lawrence. No one hurried them, and Isetta stood near the casket. I stayed back until most of the kids had gone, then Tommy and I found ourselves gazing on Lawrence. Lawrence didn't look deceased at all. His eyes were closed and he had his glasses on, which seemed kind of strange, but he was very nearsighted. Lawrence looked better dead than he ever had alive. His cheeks were rosy and seemed fatter than when I'd seen him a week ago, but there was something else very different about him.

It took me nearly a minute before I understood what it was. It was the suit and his hair. Lawrence was wearing a brown flannel pin-striped suit, just the kind he had wanted for his graduation, and his hair was cut and combed. He was wearing a white shirt with a neat paisley tie. A carnation was in the lapel of his suit, but the nicest touch of all was Lawrence's hands. They held a box containing a model for a Stearman biplane, Lawrence's favorite airplane.

Isetta edged over and said softly, "Lawrence must have built six of those planes already. They were his favorite, you know, and he wanted a suit for graduation. He never had a suit before. Now he can wear his suit and look out to see the diving board he made last summer." She wiped away some tears. "Thank you for coming. I'm sure that he would have wanted you to see his new suit." She guided us towards the front door that was never used except in summer, after giving each of us another hug.

Charley let us out after shaking our hands with his huge, callused hand. He never said a word, but I knew he was grieving for Lawrence. The new suit he was wearing was a mourning suit worn for his son. Charley could think of no other reason why he should wear a suit, and it was his tribute to Lawrence.

We went back to school for the rest of the day, but that afternoon, on the way home, I saw that the wreath on the Eastwoods' front door had been removed. Their house looked quite normal again. There were no extra cars or people about. Albert and Junior were playing with some old tires in the yard.

I thought about Lawrence in his suit, as I'd seen him that morning. I hoped that Lawrence was aware of the suit and liked it. I was glad he'd gotten his suit. In a way it was better than getting one for graduation. A graduation suit would only last a year before Lawrence would outgrow it, but he could wear his funeral suit forever.

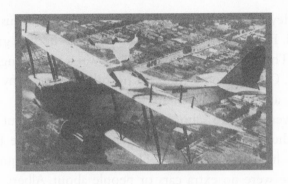

13

THE AIR CIRCUS

My Uncle Ray on the Pelletier side of the family was Dad's younger brother and a favorite relative of mine. He was young enough to be my older brother and still unmarried during my grade-school years. Uncle Ray worked in the pulp mill, but he also had a small trucking business that he operated between his pulp mill shifts. He was a jovial man who really loved children, anyone's children, and he often had neighborhood boys with him on his trucking jobs. By the time I was eight or nine, I was his kid of choice. Needless to say, I loved going places with him.

Dad was lenient about my going with Uncle Ray, seldom refusing permission. Uncle Ray had several trucks in the course of my youth, the first being a Model T Ford, which I only vaguely remember. It seemed huge to me when I was five, but it was really a tiny truck with single rear wheels and a high front seat, which had to be removed to put gasoline in the tank underneath. The truck had a split windshield so that the top half could be opened on hot days. There was nothing more exciting than to be teaming along at thirty miles an hour with the wind in my face as Uncle Ray drove hunched over the huge wooden steering wheel like Barney Oldfield in a race. Uncle Ray was a terrible teamster. He knew nothing about the mechanics of his truck and cared less. He drove by the seat of his pants and the grace of God. Grampy was likewise lost to the niceties of the gasoline engine, but had a sublime faith in God and, by extrapolation, Uncle Ray.

Uncle Ray's second truck was a 1934 Chevrolet he bought used one year. It was a mega leap forward from the Model T and had dual rear tires and a five-speed transmission. The cab was closed and had a heater, so it was warm in winter. Uncle Ray was proud of his shiny dark green new truck, and I shared his pride with him. This was the truck that Uncle Ray let me drive on occasion. Well, not really drive down roads or anything, but I did learn to move it along a few feet at a time to facilitate loading wood or hay, which was what I was doing in the summer of 1936 when I was "helping" Uncle Ray haul hay for the Penobscot Chemical Fibre Company's horses in Great Works. At that time the pulp mill was still using teams of horses around the mill yards to move pulpwood and machinery. The horses needed lots of hay in the winters.

The PCF owned or leased many of the hayfields from which its men cut hay. Most of the fields were within a few miles of the mill, and the company hired local truckers to haul the hay to the storage barns in Great Works. It was loose hay pitched onto the truck by four men. It was hot, dusty, and very itchy work for them—and for us, too—but I loved it, despite the discomfort. Uncle Ray kept me well supplied with cold Sunspot orange, which we bought each trip to the barn at the S & OK bottling works at Great Works.

Uncle Ray was a prime contractor for the haying season, but there was one problem—he worked the 12:00 A.M. to 6:00 A.M. shift at the pulp mill, and he seldom napped before going to work at midnight. He was tired. After his breakfast he could nap until about 9:30, when the hay would be dry enough to start putting it into the barn. I loved going with him and would wait impatiently for him to pick me up shortly after ten. Then it was off to the hayfield for the day.

One of the largest hayfields was on the Bradley Road. It was leased from the Jordan Lumber Company, who no longer needed the hay for its horses. It usually took a week or more to harvest that field alone. Since it was only about two miles to the pulp mill, it was a short haul, but loading and unloading often took an hour each, depending on how long we had to wait our turn.

Once we were in the field, Uncle Ray would have me take the driver's seat while he took the passenger seat. He had taught me how to steer, start the engine, and use the clutch. As we were being loaded, he slept while I moved the truck forward as the men forked on the hay. At the mill, Uncle Ray would continue his nap while we waited in line to discharge our hay. I would inch the truck forward into the barn as our turn came up, and after the hay was off-loaded, drove out the other side of the barn, where I'd wake Uncle Ray up to drive us back to the field. I felt like a giant, a real trucker, and delighted in the comments from haying crews on my skill.

So it was that the last day arrived for haying the Jordan Field. We were the only truck that Friday, hauling the scatterings of the last rakings. It was nearly August, one of those hot, sultry dog-days when lethargy weighs heavily on everyone. The loading crew was down to four men—the teamster on the horse rake and three men to load. They took turns making the load on the truck, but whatever they did was dusty, sticky, itchy work.

We were finishing up our final load of the season early that afternoon when I heard the drone of an approaching airplane. I was an airplane buff, and more than anything wanted to be a pilot some-day, so I was curious and wanted to see the plane. The drone became louder, and the hay crew started waving and shouting as the plane came over very fast and low from the southwest. I jumped from the truck just in time to see the plane come up off the river, hedge-hopping the elms growing there, to swing in a circle over the field, passing over us at about a hundred feet.

I recognized the plane as a Waco Crop Duster, from having made rubberband-powered models. Three people leaned from the plane and waved vigorously as they passed overhead. The plane flew to the far end of the field, barrel-rolled, and came back toward us. This time as it passed, a man in a white helmet and scarf leaned over the cowling and threw something out. It was a tiny parachute with a nut and paper attached. The message floated down about two hundred feet away, and one of the hay crew ran to get it. By now Uncle Ray was awake and as excited as the rest of us were.

The crew member came slowly back while reading the note.

"What does it say?" we all shouted.

"The man looked quizzical. "Wants to know which way is the wind. What the hell does that mean?" He handed Uncle Ray the note.

Uncle Ray read it, as everyone looked over his shoulder. He was puzzled, too. I also read the note. "Which way is the wind?" it said. "Point out the wind."

The plane had turned and was coming back to us. I knew instantly what it needed.

"Airplanes like to land upwind," I shouted. "Quick, we've got to make a line and hold our arms out that way." I pointed to the southwest, from which a very gentle breeze blew. I ran out from beside the truck and extended my arm. The men stood as if rooted in place until Uncle Ray yelled, "Do like Franny's doing. He knows all about airplanes." And he quickly got in line with me and extended his right arm, as I had. Now the others dashed to join us, and our line was barely formed when the plane roared overhead so low we felt the backwash of the prop.

The plane turned again towards the north and made a large circle to come back on a southwest heading. As it crossed the Bradley Road, barely clearing the utility wires, it settled abruptly and its wheels touched the ground, bounding several times before making a jouncing run towards the river. Then it slowed and turned and taxiid back to the truck.

It stopped about fifty feet away. The engine was cut. The prop made a few more revolutions and reversed itself and also stopped. Before the prop stopped the two front cockpit passengers were out of the plane and onto the wing. The short man who was last out threw out a pair of wheel chocks, ropes, and some anchor screws before jumping to the ground.

The other person was already striding towards us while removing his helmet and goggles. The white jodhpurs, shirt, and scarf were something from a Randolph Scott movie. When the helmet came off, "he" became a woman with short blond hair and a very pretty face. When "he" removed her flight jacket, she became a very attractive woman indeed, in a short-sleeved mauve blouse covering an impressive bosom. The men on the haying crew gazed with their mouths agape. In their wildest dreams they would never have expected to see a woman flyer or one so pretty.

She strode straight to Uncle Ray with her hand out. "I'm Martha," she said. "We're a barnstorming group, and we're looking for a place to fly from for the next ten days. That's Mike in the coveralls. He's our mechanic. I do the wing-walks and parachuting, and Gerry, our pilot, does the flying and owns the plane. Do you know who owns this field and whether it might be rented for a week?" She flashed Uncle Ray a smile straight from an Ipana ad.

Uncle Ray melted into speechless mush and stammered, "Er, uh, yeah. In Old Town. Lumber company. We cut hay." He looked imploringly at me. Blood was hammering in my own veins at the thought of an air circus right there before me, a flying group straight out of a Tommy Tomkins comic strip, pretty heroine and all. But I kept my cool.

I'd had to help Uncle Ray out in the past when he was flustered by women. So I stepped right up and said to Martha, "This whole field belongs to the Jordan Lumber Company in Old Town. They don't have any horses now, so they sell the hay to the PCF. That's the pulp mill across the river there. You can see it fine from the other end of this field. But you probably saw it when you flew in. Big smokestacks and piles of pulpwood."

As I spoke, the pilot joined us. He was twice Martha's age and looked like he'd not weathered life too well. He wore jodhpurs, also, greasy, grimy ones tucked into some well-scuffed-up cavalry boots. He had a really big head of curly grayish hair and a face that looked like a newly plowed field, showing unharrowed furrows of care, worry, and probably booze.

"I'm Gerry. Probably Martha told you what we need." He spoke to Uncle Ray, ignoring me. "Can you help us at all? We've got to find a place to fly out of real bad, 'cause we had a terrible week in Keene, New Hampshire. Rained all the time, fog all over, and them damned mountains nearby. We gotta earn some bucks soon." There was just a touch of desperation in his voice.

Uncle Ray recovered his voice when faced by a mere man. His big boyish grin returned, along with his courage. "Well, I think you lucked out by landing here. Two weeks ago there was hay here, two feet high, but now it's newly mown. This is a real smooth field, too. Only one problem I can see for you. That's because the Jordan Lumber Company owns the field, and that means you got to dicker with old Linny Jordan himself about renting it. And old Linny can smell dollar bills a mile away and downwind if he thinks there's a chance of getting some of them. But Franny and me is going to the PCF with this last load of hay, and we could give you a ride right to Linny's office. It ain't but two o'clock, and he'll be there even if it is Friday afternoon. Be glad to give you a ride back here, too, when I take Franny home. That is, if you want."

Gerry's newly plowed face suddenly smoothed out and even sprouted a smile. "That's damned fine of you. I never went barn-stormin' before. I do crop dusting down in Oklahoma and Texas, down South, you know. But this year all them places is blowin' away. Cotton crop ain't worth a Confederate dollar. All us crop dusters gotta earn enough to keep our planes somehow, so most of us is in the air up North here. I figured New England would be a good place to go, and you Yanks is friendly enough, but by Gawd, you do know how to hang onto a dollar. If I can make a deal for this field, you and the boy is gonna fly free whenever you want. I'll take that ride to town with you."

And there I was, squeezed in between Uncle Ray and Gerry, headed for Old Town. Gerry smelled awfully rank, of grease, gasoline, and sweat, but it was a true glory ride—right next to a real air pilot. I hoped one of my friends would see me, but it was too hot a day. They were all swimming. We let Gerry out at the lumber company with instructions to wait for us. It would take us an hour to unload our hay.

It was a long hour for me, despite the fact that we didn't have to wait a minute to unload. I just wanted to see that air circus again. It was making up to a thunderstorm by the time we picked up Gerry. His face looked like it had already been rained on—hard. But he had some papers in his hand, which was a good sign that he had been successful in making a deal for the use of the field. After he got into the truck, he turned to Uncle Ray and said laconically, "Gawd, I thought them rednecks down in Georgia and Alabama was hard to deal with, but Mr. Linny Jordan wrote the book on closing a deal. I'm gonna be lucky to make enough money for fuel to fly to the next stop with this contract, but I ain't got no choice. I'm down to about one re-fueling and a few days' meals, if we don't eat much. He's gonna get half of every ticket I sell, which means I gotta raise my prices to five dollars a person, which no one will pay, or fly short flights and make six dollars a flight, which ain't enough."

Uncle Ray said nothing, but I could tell he was thinking by the way he gripped the steering wheel. At the Milford bridge, he kind of cleared his throat and asked, "How much you charge per person, and how many can you carry per flight?"

"I get three dollars a head, and I carry four at a time. But my parachuting and wing-walking flights don't bring in dime one. They just attract the crowd, so I can get passengers. And I've got expenses like the leaflets that I drop to tell where we are. They cost to get printed, ya know. And I need 3,000 or 4,000 of those. I don't know. Maybe I'd best go to Bangor and pay field rental rates at the airport there."

Uncle Ray said no more until we got back to the plane, where we found that Mike and Martha had set up a little pup tent and made a screened area under the right wing. The plane was tied down to the screws in the ground, and there were chocks front and rear on both wheels. Martha came bouncing up to the truck. "Can we stay, or do I have to take down my wing tent?" she asked. And then she added, "Did you find a place to eat, or am I going to walk into

Bradley for something from the store—if there is one?"

Gerry replied to these queries morosely. "We can stay, but it don't look too good. Maybe we can hitch into Old Town for a meal. Any good places to eat there, Ray? Cheap, I mean."

Uncle Ray seemed to come out of the fog of thought he'd been in and said, "I'll give you a ride into town after I take Franny home, but first I'd kind of like to read your contract, if you don't mind. Might be some way to beat ol' Linny."

Gerry unfolded the papers and placed them on the hood of the truck. Uncle Ray read them aloud, haltingly. He wasn't a strong reader, but the contract was clear enough. Gerry would charge three dollars a person and Linny got half. To keep Gerry honest, Linny would provide numbered tickets, and the tickets sold had to agree with the money taken in. There were no other fees and no mention of wing-walking and parachuting. Also, one of Linny's men would be on hand each day to kind of keep an eye on things. It looked pretty airtight.

Uncle Ray drummed his fingers on the hood as he read. After some thought he said to Gerry, "Looks to me like you only got to share if you charge for the rides."

Gerry snorted, "Of course, but I can't fly people for free. Any dummy can see that."

Uncle Ray ignored the insult. "Well, seems like to me you ought to charge for the stunting and offer a free ride to anyone who buys a ticket to watch the stunts."

Martha's eyes widened then turned into narrow slits as she looked at Uncle Ray with real respect. There was something more than just Uncle Ray's smarts there, too.

"Mike, I think Ray's onto something," She flashed Uncle Ray a ravishing smile and put her head close to his. "This sounds do-able, Ray, but what about Linny's man? He's gonna blow the whistle on that little scheme in jig time."

Uncle Ray pursed his lips and leaned a little towards Martha, looking down her blouse as he remarked, "Linny only pays minimum wage. That's $3.20 a day. I bet if you explained to whoever is sent out that you'd be willing to part with a ten-spot each day for him to keep quiet until the last day, that feller would take kindly to the idea. I don't really feel it's crooked. Linny'd take any advantage he could git. In fact, he'd skin a fart for four cents, when most of his ilk would want a dime. Worth a try, anyhow."

Now Gerry was excited. "By Gawd, I bet we could pull it off. We'll print our flyers to say, 'See the air circus and get a ride in the airplane for $3.00.' That way we ain't saying the ride is free or the viewing is free. It's $3.00 if you want to do both. Might just work, and if Linny comes by himself, we'll give him a free ride. Ray, you're a genius even if you are a Yankee."

Uncle Ray grinned modestly and ogled Martha some more. Martha noticed.

"It would be our pleasure to treat you to dinner with us tonight, and I wouldn't mind going to a dance, if there's any around here. I sure love to dance, and dancin' with a big fella like you is real nice," Martha said in a truly coy Southern belle lisp, halting briefly between each word and thrusting her bosom ever closer to Uncle Ray's face.

Uncle Ray was interested, even though he was all red-colored, but he started stammering about not being much of a dancer, so I helped him out by telling Martha that there was dancing every weekend at the Villa Vaughn on Pushaw Pond, and that the pavilion was real nice.

"Oh, that sounds like so much fun. I'd love to go to the dance there, but I'd have to have you drive me, Ray, unless there's a taxi service. And don't worry about not dancing well. Dancing is something I enjoy very much—among other things—and I feel lucky to go with a man as handsome as you are—and smart." Uncle Ray was trapped, hog-tied, and tongue-tied, but managed to offer anyone who wanted to go a ride to the Villa Vaughn.

Gerry and Mike could see how the wind was blowing, being flyers and all, but Martha added a little clarification. "I'd be just delighted to go with you—ALONE—Ray. I'm sure Mike and Gerry here are too tired to go anywhere, and besides, they have work to do on the plane, don't you, fellas? And I've never been on a date in a truck before. I feel as girlish as when I was the Cotton Queen in high school. I really do!"

Well, I went home quite excited about the air circus and the pretty wing-walker. I had a promise of a free plane ride on Monday evening. I was worried about that, though, because I couldn't see Dad letting me ride in an airplane. But Uncle Ray said he would fix that up—just don't say anything to anyone about Martha.

On Monday night Uncle Ray came over right after supper and asked Dad if I could go with him to watch the wing-walking. Of course, my siblings wanted to go, too, but there wasn't room in the truck. Dad silenced the uproar by agreeing to take them later to see the air show, while I went ahead with Uncle Ray.

It was only 6:30 when we got to the field. There weren't a lot of people there yet, and Martha came over immediately and gushed all over Uncle Ray, remarking at how quickly he had learned to dance and all and how much he was a gentleman that a girl would want to please in every way. She said she was looking forward to the rest of the week because of him.

Uncle Ray just grinned, shuffled his feet, and remarked that dancing with Martha was something no man would want to pass over, and that he was looking forward to seeing more of her, too.

Just about then three young guys from French Island came along and wanted to buy tickets to see the show and get a free ride. Martha handled ticket sales from a card table set up near the plane. The guys were a little hesitant at first about flying, but Martha joshed them about it, explaining that she wing-walked, parachuted, and did other stunts like that every day, and surely such strong men wouldn't want to be shown up by "itty-bitty shy, helpless me."

They had partaken of considerable liquid bravery. The booze and Martha's blatant sexiness stiffened their spines, so to speak, and they bought tickets. Gerry escorted them to the plane and got them aboard. Then he turned to me. "There's room for you, Franny. You want to go?"

I looked up at Uncle Ray, who nodded, and Gerry swung me

up into the cockpit of the Waco. It wasn't what I had expected. There were no padded seats, only two wide planks across the fuselage struts of the plane, well down in the fuselage. Two of the guys were seated backwards to me as I took my seat beside the third, who was looking very worried. None of us could see out of the cockpit, but we could see down, right through the floor where the fabric had been cut away in an elongated circle. A heavy wire mesh was secured over the hole, and we could see the tubes of the fuselage through the mesh.

Mike clambered up and secured our seat belts and the little harnesses that held our shoulders back against a six-inch-wide band of steel that was bolted to each side of the frame. We were ready to go. Mike went around front to the prop and awaited Gerry's call of "Contact!" The engine exploded into life. The noise was deafening and fumes rolled into the cockpit. The fellow next to me started coughing and yelling that he had changed his mind. He clawed at the seat belt, but it was too late. The engine revved, and the plane slowly started over the field. Then we were pounding roughly, bouncing and swaying over the turf, which I could see racing backwards beneath my feet. Then there was a moment of quiet, followed by a couple of sharp jolts as the wheels hit turf again, and then we lifted off.

It was sheer delight for me. I could see the ground below me falling away as we climbed in a steep curve to the northeast. There was the river just under us as we soared upwards over French Island several hundred feet below. I saw cars, houses, and people suddenly miniaturized before my eyes. And there was the bridge in Old Town, strange-looking when viewed from above. The city green and bandstand slid by, followed by the pie plate mill and the woolen mills, and now we were over Indian Island. I was enraptured by the view, with no sense at all of height, just pure freedom.

My seat partner, however, was petrified with fear. His eyes were squinched tight, and he was a ghastly shade of green. Both hands gripped the rim of the cockpit as he tried to pull himself up. But I couldn't waste time with him and turned to my view again.

Now we were well over Stillwater and flying down the Stillwater River above the University of Maine and Orono. Over Orono the plane bounced upward and then down in the mother of all "Yes, Ma'ams." We seemed to slide sideways as the pilot recovered from the rough air, only to hit another "air pocket." My companions were holding the planks of their seats in terror. The man next to me had his mouth open in a scream I couldn't hear over the engine. Then we were over High Head, with more rocking as we climbed. When we passed over the PCF, the piles of pulpwood seemed immense, even from the air, and I could see a ballgame going on at PCF Field.

Now we wheeled right over the Penobscot again, over Bradley and the enormous dam, and then started to descend for the landing. But Gerry gave us one last thrill, suddenly climbing fast and high into a great wheeling turn steep enough so that I was crushed by my partner as centrifugal force threw him against me, pinning me to the fuselage tubes. Now I could see the sky through the floor, and the town of Milford was standing edgewise. What a thrilling ride! And then, as we leveled out and came in for a landing, my seat partner lost it. He let go of the cockpit rim, leaned forward towards his friends, and covered them both in a shower of beer and supper.

As the wheels thumped the ground—once, twice, and after a prolonged leap, the third time—we rolled to a stop where we had started fifteen minutes before. The engine coughed to a halt, belching a huge cloud of oily smoke that caused the second guy to lose his guts. Most of the puke went out through the "porthole" onto the ground. But Mike, who was helping the other two out of the plane, swore over the mess, saying, "I hope you bastards choke on your own bile. Now I'll have to wash out the whole damned cockpit before the next flight."

I climbed out as fast as I could to get away from the smell, and the three men alighted to the jeers of their peers, who were waiting for the crestfallen heroes.

That was my first flight in an airplane. I was the only kid in town to have flown in an airplane. Dad was torn between being sore at Uncle Ray and proud of me. He wouldn't have gone on a flight for anything, but he was sure proud of my flying. Uncle Ray never did go for a flight, although he told me years later that Martha had promised some high-altitude acrobatics not advertised in the pamphlets they printed and dropped.

The air circus did as well during their stay as they had the whole season to date. The weather held warm and muggy, encouraging people to come out to watch Martha dangle perilously from the top wing as the plane flew over the field upside down, and to try flying themselves. The double parachuting of both Martha and Mike ensured good turnouts each evening.

I don't know how or when Linny Jordan realized he'd been scammed, but he still ended up with a hundred dollars for the week's rent. It seemed like pretty good money to me.

Airplanes were still rare in that part of Maine, and it was a memorable summer. As for the daring young woman on the flying machine, Uncle Ray once commented that she danced quite beautifully and intermissioned even better.

14

Puppy Love

My little dog Tykey was the most precious thing I had ever owned. Tykey was the runt pup of a spring litter from a pedigreed, dazzling white Spitz mother. Mitzie, as she was named, was owned by a friend of my father's and was his constant companion, a truly pampered little one-year-old bitch. Her owner had not intended for her to have a litter that spring, but Mitzi escaped her owner long enough to foil his attempts to keep her virginal. To be frank, Mitzi, although she was as white and pure as the snow, did what snow does. She drifted. A brief affair with a tiny male champagne-colored French poodle that lived next door resulted in a litter of seven tiny gold and white puppies, of which Tykey was the tiniest. The only consolation for her owner lay in the fact that Mitzi's lover was also pedigreed, and the litter that resulted was salable because the puppies were so cute.

I saw the puppies for the first time when they were about two weeks old. Dad's friend was also his auto mechanic. Dad's mechanical abilities had never got beyond being able to lift the hood covers on either side of the engine. He could change a tire, provided there were no women around to hear him swear, and he knew that gas went into the little round hole with a cover on the hood. Otherwise, Dad was auto-illiterate. He depended on his friend Harry for any service on our Model B Ford.

The Ford needed a new muffler because Dad had driven over County Road during the spring thaw and hit a boulder pushed up by a frost heave. All of our neighbors replaced the mufflers on their cars themselves, but not Dad. Removing and replacing a muffler, to him, was akin to a doctor removing and replacing a liver. It was high-tech stuff, so he took the Ford to Harry.

I liked to go to Harry's because I liked both Harry and his dog. Mitzi could do lots of tricks. Harry had great patience with dogs and had trained her to sit up and beg, to fetch, to play dead, and most amazing to me, to walk on her front legs. She loved to perform and would do all her tricks over and over. When I found out that Dad was going to Harry's for the evening while the Ford got a new muffler, I begged to go along.

Mitzi had come bouncing up when we drove into the drive, and she literally led us to her puppies, which were in a clothes basket behind the cast iron kitchen range. She got in the basket, curling herself around the pile of pups, and they immediately sorted themselves out and headed for a nipple as Mitzi stretched to accommodate them. There were four puppies about the size of a small rat, and Tykey. Three of the four largest were nearly all white with just a few tiny golden spots. The other was a mirror image in color, being all gold with a few white spots.

But Tykey stood out. Besides being the smallest, he was the prettiest. He was white with a big golden patch around his right eye and ear. His front legs were also white, but his left hind leg was golden, as was half his rump, right up to and around his tail, which was white. His eyes were open and he had tiny, round black puppy eyes that matched his black puppy nose perfectly. But what made Tykey stand out was his hair. Whereas his siblings (all females) had Spitz hair, long and sleek, Tykey had fluffy poodle hair that was a mass of curls and ringlets. He was gorgeous, and I never wanted anything so much in my life as I wanted that puppy.

Harry and Dad went to the garage for the muffler transplant. I stayed in the kitchen and played with Tykey. He was too tiny and weak to get and keep a nipple of his own. Every time he found one and started his mother's milk flowing, a bigger sister pushed him away and latched onto his faucet. Poor Tykey whimpered and fought valiantly but got little to drink until I picked up all the siblings and gave Tykey sole access to Mitzi.

To her credit, she seemed to know that here was a child who needed extra love, for she licked him constantly as he sucked. He seemed overwhelmed by all the care and kneaded fiercely with his tiny front feet as he nursed. Sometimes even his hind feet kicked. Tykey drank until his belly bulged and then went to sleep with a nipple clenched firmly in his mouth. I put the sisters back in the basket and went out to plead with Dad and Harry for Tykey.

Dad was not an animal lover. He was an animal eater. Any animal that could not serve as food on his table was beneath his ken. It was not that he was ever cruel to pet animals, but he tolerated puppies, abided dogs, and really disliked cats. We had a cat, Brownie, who gave Dad wide berth, never getting within six feet of him. I knew I would have to talk up a real story to convince Dad that I should have Tykey. I also wondered if Harry would part with his pups.

Fortunately, the muffler transplant was going well. Harry was under the car on a grease-encrusted creeper hanging the new organ on the head pipe. I knew it was going well because there was a steady stream of swearing pouring like exhaust from under the car as Harry tightened clamps. The old muffler lay by the car, twisted and battered by the boulder.

I squatted down to peer under the car to negotiate with Harry before I tackled Dad.

"Those are awful cute puppies. What are you going to do with so many?" I queried.

Harry grunted as he worked the ratchet wrench. "Probably sell 'em all. Got one good dog now. My wife don't want no puppies pooping all over the house. Be lots of dog poop soon's they begin to run around. Probably sell 'em all then, if they's weaned." Harry paused to heave a bent and rusted U-clamp towards the lower part of a trashcan.

"How much do puppies like that cost?" I hoped in my heart that Harry was going to do the generous thing and offer to give me one, but Harry was a pragmatist. He knew he had an interested customer.

"Going price for bitches of crossbreeds is three dollars, but them pups is from pedigreed parents with papers, and they're a good cross. Poodles and Spitzes are smart and make the best pets. I figure I can get five dollars for the bitches, probably eight for the male, even though he is the runt. He's the cutest and prettiest. You like to have a pup?"

My heart sank. Harry had noticed that Tykey was the best of the litter.

I noticed Dad coming in from the garden, where he had been talking to Harry's wife, whom we always called Mrs. Harry, probably because her name was Hortense.

"Well, I always wanted a puppy, and I sure like the boy dog. I already named him Tykey 'cause he looks like a dog in our school reading book called Tykey. I haven't talked to Dad yet. He doesn't like pets too much, though. Eight dollars is a lot of money," I added with a very audible sigh for Harry's benefit.

"Eight dollars?" Dad had heard us. "Eight dollars for what? Eight dollars is a lot of money."

I grimaced at the floor, knowing I wouldn't get Tykey. But I decided to play out my hand in a bluff.

"Oh, I was asking Harry what he's going to do with all those puppies. He's going to sell all of them. Five dollars for the girl dogs and eight for the boy dog. I guess we couldn't get one at those prices, but I always wanted a puppy. Someday I'll probably buy one for myself," I said with a cheerful, expectant look, this time hoping that Dad would surprise me with sudden benevolence.

But it wasn't to be. Dad looked at me as if I had my head

stuffed with oatmeal and it was running out both ears.

"You can buy any dog you want, if you got the money. Me, I don't throw money away on pets. They cost too much to buy, and then you have to feed 'em. Those are cute pups, though. Your mother would sure think they were cuddly."

For a moment Dad's statement went over my head and I almost missed the significance of what he had said.

"You mean, if I could get the money, I could buy a puppy? Really?"

Dad looked perplexed for a moment, trying to recall his statement fully. He got just a bit flushed, as he often did when he was thinking.

"Yeah, I guess if you had the money, I'd let you have a dog. You'd have to take care of it, though. Clean up the poop and housebreak it. Have to see whether your mother would approve, too. I wouldn't want just any dog, though. A small one—like Harry's got here—would be okay."

I felt gleeful and my plan was already forming. Harry had tightened the last clamp and rolled out from under the Ford. He was red with muffler rust and soot. I didn't wait.

"Dad said if I could get the money, I could buy a puppy. I want the boy puppy. The one I call Tykey. How soon before he gets sold?" I wanted that puppy more each minute.

Harry grinned through his rust and soot. He looked like the end man in a minstrel show, his teeth all shiny white, just ready to do a tap and song number. But it was really me that wanted to do the tap and song.

"That Jeezely muffler was a tough one, Emile. I got to charge you three bucks for putting on the new one, plus the muffler and two clamps. Come to about ten dollars altogether. But I tell you what. If Franny here wants that male puppy, I'll let him have it for five dollars, to kind of make up for the muffler, you know."

Dad was looking like he'd been sucking on a lemon, whether from the muffler costs or the idea that he might find himself living in the same house with a dog, I wasn't sure, but he counted out eight ones and some change and paid Harry. He got into the Ford, still without saying a word, and started it up. The roar was gone. It idled with a rocking purr, like a cat full of warm milk. Dad smiled. His beloved Model B had come through the transplant and was whole once more. The prospect of a dog in the future could be faced when it happened.

He nodded at me. "Get in. It's past your bedtime already. Did a good job on the car, Harry. And thanks for the offer about the dog. Let me know if you get an offer on it." He backed the Ford out of the garage and we went home.

I didn't say a word to Mama until the next morning, after Dad had gone to the store, then I told her about Tykey. I described him in glowing terms, telling her how much she would like to have him. She listened soberly, but I could tell I was making points because Mama's eyes got very soft looking, like they did the times I brought her a Bartlett pear from O. G. Morrin's Fruit and Confectioner's Store. Mama loved fresh pears. She used to say that she thought that the Bible was wrong about the apple and Eve. No one would be that tempted by an apple, but they would by a Bartlett pear. Anyway, when I finished, she said, "I think I would like to have a Tykey dog. Maybe you can get him. Does Grampy Pelletier know you want a dog? He loves dogs and is always telling about the dogs he had when he was a boy."

My heart leapt. Mama and I could often come to understandings without ever really talking about things. I had thought about Grampy immediately the evening before when Dad said I could have a dog if I could get the money to buy it. Now Mama was giving me tacit permission to tell Grampy about Tykey. I often visited Grampy after school in the flag station in Old Town where he put the gates up and down for the Maine Central Railroad. He worked the three-to-eleven shift, six days a week. Twice a week he and I went to the movies in the evening while Dad manned the station.

On our walk to the movies that Wednesday night, I told Grampy all about Tykey. While we waited for the movie to start, he asked if Mama minded if I had a dog. He smiled his benignly enigmatic smile when I told him Mama had said I should tell him about Tykey.

"Your mama is a very fine lady. Very smart. Smartest thing Emile ever do when he marry her. Is good t'ing you tell Grampy about puppy. Little boys need puppies dog. Don't talk no more to your daddy about puppy. Me and Mama fix to have puppy for you."

It was a wonderful movie—Buck Jones in something or other—but I never heard a word because my head was filled with Tykey. I knew he was mine as sure as I knew the sun would come up in the morning. It was a warm April night as I walked back to the flag station with my hand in Grampy's big callused hand. Just before we got to the door, Grampy squeezed my hand hard.

"Remember, don't say no t'ing to you daddy about puppy dogs. He do what his papa say for him to do. He very good boy, too."

We lingered longer that evening in the flag station as Dad and Grampy talked. Just before we left, Grampy said casually to Dad, "On Sunday when we go for ride in afternoon, I t'ink we go by Sunrise Farm. I like Sunrise Farm in springtime. Maybe I buy pig from Mr. Mayhew at Sunrise Farm. Is good time to buy pig in April. Get small pig and take home in car. Small pigs is cheap. Okay we go to Sunrise Farm?"

Dad readily agreed to go pigging, as we called our annual search for a couple of pigs. Dad loved to go pigging. To go to Sunrise Farm, we had to drive right by Harry's house. Dad had been snookered but good. I wanted to hug Grampy and run the gates up and down a few times out of sheer glee.

Sunday was a lovely, warm April day. After mass I went to Grampy's, as usual. My uncles, aunts, and cousins were all there, filling up on my Aunt Edna's coffee and doughnuts, homemade bread, and other good stuff that she never tired of making. There was the usual loud talk and laughter of people who enjoyed each other. Dad mentioned that he was taking Grampy pigging in the afternoon, and Uncle Ed asked Dad to look for a good pig for him, also—maybe two, if the price was right on some sizable shoats. Uncle Ray put in an order for one. I began to worry about where I was going to put the puppy I expected to get.

Our dinner back at our house was one of Mama's better ones. Stewed pork chops and dumplings in a thick gravy with mashed potatoes, buttered carrots and pickled beets for veggies, and butterscotch meringue pie for dessert. Grampy loved Mama's cooking. After every meal he would push his chair back, take the silver toothpick out of his vest pocket, lean back, and say as he wielded his toothpick, "That very fine dinner, Fanny. You make cook just like my Dorilda. Four daughters I got. Nobody cook so good as you, like Dorilda. Emile very lucky man to marry cook like his mother." Mama would always thank him, and I could see she liked it when Grampy praised her cooking.

Grampy paid his compliments as usual, Mama cleaned up the dishes, and my siblings went off to catechism class. I was excused to go pigging. At Mr. Mayhew's we found four Chester White brood sows with about fifteen piglets each. We hit the bonanza. Dad and Grampa dickered over the four dollars that Mayhew was asking for pigs from the litter with the tiniest pigs and settled for a price of three dollars apiece. They were as cute as piglets always are—all pink and white and full to the ears with squeals. Mr. Mayhew packed them two to a bag in old grain sacks and tied them on the Model B's chromed baggage carrier. After an hour at the farm we left for home. I was beginning to worry. I didn't have my puppy.

On the way home Dad was gleeful. He'd gotten pigs for everyone on the first stab at pigging for the season. We had almost passed Harry's house when Grampy held up his hand.

"Emile," he said, "Isn't that Harry Martin's place? I not see him for long while. He don't stop no more my flag station. I t'ink we stop, say hello. Harry one fine man, him. Mebbe he sick. We stop."

Dad never questioned his father. Grampy's request was Dad's command. He stopped and backed up the few yards to Harry's drive and pulled into it. Harry and Mrs. Harry were in the backyard garden with hoes in their hands. They came to the car as we all got out. The pigs on the back started squealing when the car stopped. They must have preferred riding. Harry walked right up to Dad.

"Come to get that puppy, have ye, Emile? He's growing like crazy. I believe he might even catch up to the little bitches." Harry was effusive at the prospect of five dollars. He turned to Grampa.

"Nice to see you, Joe. Been plannin' on stoppin' by the station, but been awful busy with lots of cars to fix. Franny would like to have a puppy I got here. You wanna see him? Hortense, go git that pup."

Grampy was as smooth as brushed velvet as he manipulated the conversation when Mrs. Harry came back with Tykey. No one could resist the puppy. He'd grown enough in a week that he could do a tottering walk on the grass. He nuzzled anyone who held him. Even Dad smiled and stroked the little guy. Harry let us look and hold, then he said, "I got to tell you, Emile. Harry Boynton's taken a liking to this pup, but I told him you had first refusal. You want him, you got him for five bucks, like I said." Harry waited.

Dad never had a chance to say a word. Grampy had Tykey in his huge callused hands. He gently scratched the ears. He turned to Harry.

"I buy doggy. Makes for good pet my grandson, Franny, here. Franny very good boy, him. Go to movie all time and read me words from picture show. Emile, I t'ink is good for little boys to have puppy for play and care. Is okay by you Franny have puppy?"

Dad grinned. I think he suspected he'd been scammed, but he wouldn't admit it. He just said, "Pa, Ma always said you was slicker than goose grease in getting what you want. Go ahead and buy Franny a puppy."

So I went home with Tykey. He weighed about a pound that day. I double-loved every ounce of him. I couldn't sleep that night with him down in the kitchen in a shoebox by the stove, so as soon as Dad and Mama went to bed, I went down and got him. He slept curled up under my right arm all night and every night after that.

In no time Tykey became my shadow. It was a wonderful summer with Tykey. I had him until late July, when he got run over by a car and instantly killed. It was the last Sunday in July, a sultry hot day, when it happened.

Mama had invited Aunt Enid over for Sunday dinner. She was the strange child in Dad's family. A spinster, she was sour and finicky about lots of things, two of them being cats and dogs. She just plain couldn't stand pets.

After dinner Dad drove us all to catechism class, because Mama said it was too hot for us to walk. Later, Dad decided that a Sunday drive would be good for them all, so he and Mama and Aunt Enid and my little sister Anna piled in the Ford. Aunt Enid loved Sunday rides. So did Tykey, who set to racing around the car, barking like mad and jumping onto the running board. He was about half grown now, and cute as a button with his little doughnut tail curled over his back. He never walked—Tykey pranced and strutted.

Dad got out to put Tykey in the house, but then he decided to take him along, knowing they'd meet us on our way home from catechism class and he could leave Tykey with us. But I'd stopped at the flag station for a visit with Grampy, so I wasn't with Paul and Ellen when they met Dad on the Old Town–Milford bridge.

Aunt Enid was already fussing up a storm about having a dog in the car. She thought car rides should be dignified. "No gawking and talking," she told us. "People will stare." But that's why we went on Sunday drives—so we could gawk and talk and stare back. Dad handed Tykey to Paul and told him to take Tykey home. They drove off.

We didn't own a leash. Tykey didn't need one at home. Paul put him on the sidewalk and off they skipped, with Tykey yapping at their heels. They didn't even make it across the bridge before Tykey spotted some pigeons and made a dash for them, right under the wheels of an oncoming car. He was crushed in an instant. Paul and Ellen were horror-struck. The driver stopped and tried to console them. Paul carried Tykey's lifeless body home.

An hour later I got home. I was grief-stricken. We found a small wooden box and laid Tykey out in it, wrapped in a towel. Our parents got home about that time and Dad took us to a spot out under the wild cherry tree, where we buried Tykey with full honors and many tears.

But my story has a happy ending of sorts. Harry Martin came to the house about two months after Tykey had been killed. He had Mitzi with him. It seems Mrs. Harry didn't like dogs any more than Aunt Enid had. Once Harry sold off the litter, Hortense gave him an ultimatum: it was her or Mitzi. There was no room in their house for both. Harry knew about Tykey, so he brought me Mitzi.

If I'd been him, I would have chosen Mitzi over Hortense. I fell in love with her instantly. She was a queenly dog and we bonded in no time. I had her for five years, and she was my shadow whenever I was home. She never replaced the first puppy love I lavished on Tykey, but she certainly eased the ache.

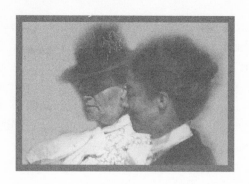

15

THE DIFFERENCE BETWEEN 'EM

Politics in Milford during the '30s were intense and personal. Most of the townspeople were registered Republicans, and the Republican party drew a large majority in every state and national election. Milford returns could always be expected to show at least an 80 percent return for any Republican who ran for office.

There were a few registered Democrats, but they kept a low profile. In every election there were always some votes cast for the Democrats, usually far more than the number of votes who were registered Democrats. These votes were attributed to a number of the voters who were listed as Independents, but who were suspected by mainline Republicans of being radicals of the worst kind. Some of these were even suspected—and in some cases openly accused—of being socialists or even communists. Matty Jackson was one of these.

Matty was an avowed radical and made no bones about his convictions. In the daily forum meetings around the potbellied stove in Spruce's Store, Matty extolled the virtues of Franklin Delano Roosevelt as though FDR were the new messiah. In Matty's view, the National Recovery Act would lift the nation by its bootstraps from the depths of the depression. The "New Deal" would be the New Testament of the Roosevelt era. It would assure the working man of an adequate wage and dignity and take the country back from robber barons like the Rockefellers and Henry Ford.

The fact that Matty Jackson had never in anyone's memory done a day's work in his life didn't stop him from considering himself a workingman and downtrodden member of the working class. Among Matty's ideas for the betterment of the country's socioeconomic growth was an ardent and vocal belief in trade unionism, particularly as manifested by the newly formed CIO. Matty also gave strong support to the United Mine Workers, and he considered John L. Lewis to be a John the Baptist, crying in the wilderness of social and economic discontent fostered by the rapacious giants of the industrial revolution.

These opinions didn't endear Matty to the Republican political leaders who ran the town. Matty did have a few disciples of his own, but for the most part they were the same few who appeared at the town office periodically looking for assistance to feed their families. Poorly educated, and chronically unemployed, they were scorned by the town fathers as indolent and unworthy of the welfare help the laws required the town to provide.

Matty's political views were particularly galling to the town fathers because of his own lack of steady employment and his easygoing lifestyle. Also, he wasn't a native. He'd been born and raised in Greenfield, a small and dying neighboring town to the east. Matty came to Milford in his late thirties to take up residence in a series of homes where he boarded until such time as he had worn out his welcome.

Since he had no steady income, he usually made some arrangement to work out his board and room by doing chores and "fixing" things for his host family. For a while after he showed up in Milford people vied to have him for a boarder because Matty could "fix" anything. He seemed endowed with an innate ability to understand mechanical things, and he loved to put his mind to the problem of a broken radio, a leaky faucet, a failed water pump, or a cranky car. He was considered to be a genius with all things mechanical.

But when it came to the more mundane chores, such as wood splitting, gardening, or shoveling snow, Matty had a recurring and convenient spinal problem. A good-sized snowstorm could prostrate Matty for several days, confining him to bed in great distress. The first sign of a coming storm was a signal for Matty to start leaning forward while reaching for his back and moaning with grimaces. The first snowflake sent him to bed, where his recovery seemed to coincide with the speed with which his present host or hostess cleared the snow from their premises. Gardening in spring and summer elicited similar attacks. Matty's hosts would endure him until he had repaired their mechanical problems, and a little longer for decency's sake, and then he would be sent packing.

When Matty had nothing to fix, he would read. He was a prodigious reader, with a boundless appetite for books, magazines, and newspapers. It did not matter to Matty that the papers he read were several days old or the periodicals several months past new. He read them. He borrowed books from anyone who would lend them to him, took meticulous care of the borrowed works, and returned them promptly. Matty's choice of reading material was all-encompassing. There was no subject too dull, too esoteric, or too plebeian for his mind. He read whatever came his way, and everyone lent him books or gave him their old magazines and newspapers.

This reading habit also offended the elders of the town, because whatever topic of discussion came up around the potbellied stove, Matty would jump right in, and if the veracity of his input was challenged, he would be ready with chapter and verse to verify his authority. He managed at one time or another to embarrass each of the town fathers. They considered him an uppity ne'er-do-well.

So Matty survived, but his life must have been a lonely one. He had no relatives in town and only marginally interacted with his fellow townsmen. He seemed to have no intimate friends, certainly no lady friends. Occasionally, when Matty was absent from the stove sessions, Matty's lovelife was discussed. No one could remember Matty to ever have had a liaison of any kind with the opposite sex. This led some of the more sophisticated of the group to suggest that, perhaps, Matty was, you know, "funny." At such times a pall of silence would settle on the group for awhile as everyone pondered this possibility. The suggestion that Matty might have homosexual tendencies was often tendered in such a way that it was an open offer for anyone to confirm the suspicion, but to so do might incriminate oneself in the minds of the others present, so while speculation persisted, no facts were offered.

I first met Matty when I was in seventh grade. I was doing gardening chores for the McClendons, where Matty boarded. Alec McClendon had recently had a heart attack that left him unable to do any but very light physical tasks. His wife Mary was New Brunswick Scots, a devout Catholic, an elected town clerk on the Republican ticket, and the childless wife of an Irish immigrant who was as orange as she was green. Mary was tiny, not quite five feet tall. She was sixty-five years old then, wore gold-rimmed "granny" glasses, and was always attired in long, rusty black dresses that came to the top of her high, laced shoes. The black was in mourning for her dear mother (God rest her soul) who had died forty years before, shortly after the death of Mary's only child, a son. Mary had been in perpetual mourning dress for her son and her mother (God rest her soul) ever since.

Alec had built a house for them in 1890, hoping to fill its rooms with children, but now Mary ran it as a boardinghouse. The deaths seemed to have cast a pall over the marriage, and they had drifted into a polite armistice, addressing each other when necessary as Mr. and Mrs. McClendon when alone, and through a third person when one was present.

Shortly after the boardinghouse opened, a young Irish woman came to board with them. Megan O'Reilly was as devout as Mary, but she was big and strong. She was also plain and an orphan, and had come to America under the auspices of the Catholic orphanage system, which often sent out parcels of hapless children to a local parish where they could be chosen by some childless couple.

Megan had been too old and too big and plain to be chosen for adoption, and she had been passed over several times. When she was old enough, she was sent out to marry a recently widowed man with a family of six children. But even this man in his great need for a mother for his family turned Megan down flat, saying to Mother Superior, "Gawd, woman, Oi'm not dead ye know. I'd feel like Oi'm in bed with me brother. She's that plain, she is." Mother Superior wasn't surprised by his refusal and hoped that now Megan might be induced to devote her life to the Sisters of Mercy and the Catholic Church.

Instead, Megan took her few belongings and the five dollars that each orphan was given when he or she left the orphanage, and took a room at the McClendons' where she shared a room with another girl. Mary took her on as cook and maid. She remained there for the rest of her life, with time out to cook in the homes of various affluent families in town.

Now there were no boarders at the McClendons'—just Alec, Mary, and Megan. When Matty, in desperation, came knocking for a room, Mary took him in, but only until he could find another place. Matty performed as usual, mending the items that had been neglected during Alec's illness and reading Mary's periodicals. Mary took five newspapers, both morning and evening Bangor and Portland papers, plus the *Boston Post*. I came in to do the gardening and sometimes the woodpile.

Two houses down the street from the McClendons' there was a house where two sisters lived. The older sister and owner of the house was a widow of a year, and her younger sister was a spinster. The widow had a small pension, and her sister was an expert seamstress, so together they managed quite well. Neighbors helped them through snowstorms, and they both gardened extensively in summer. They were both in their fifties, and their only relative was a brother in western New York.

Matty had arrived at the McClendons' in early summer, and sometimes during the evening he would go for a short stroll. The sisters often sat on their front porch in their rockers, the younger basting a hem or stitching in a lining while the older read. Passersby often stopped to sit and chat with them on the porch for a bit. Eventually Matty received an invitation to sit, also. He was reluctant at first, but could think of no plausible reason why he shouldn't, so he accepted and passed a pleasant half-hour with the sisters.

Although the sisters weren't young, they were attractive women with youthful faces and stylish wardrobes. Both women had matronly figures, but the seamstress's skill made them seem younger than they were. They were, in a word, pretty. Matty—who was tall and lank, with a long, narrow face and head and a sallow complexion—seemed incongruous sitting there on the porch with them. He wore an ill-fitting black suit that was threadbare, shiny, and a size too small for him. He had an aquiline nose and thinning black hair that hung greasy and limp to his collar. I always thought he looked like Uriah Heep in *David Copperfield,* but the sisters apparently found him interesting, for they were often seen talking and laughing happily in conversation with Matty.

By fall it was evident that something more than a platonic relationship had developed between the widow and Matty. Now on good evenings they were seen to leave the porch and stroll to the park or even to the river, where they walked the paths that lovers took. The seamstress remained on the porch busy with her work.

Talk around the potbellied stove often turned to Matty, now. He still came in each day as before, at seven in the morning and again for the evening mail. He was as gabby as ever about all topics except his new friendship. Any attempts to elicit a comment about the widow were deftly turned aside. But the relationship continued to grow. Now the two shopped together mid-morning, Mrs. Hyatt making the purchases and Matty graciously carrying them home for her.

At the end of September, Matty left the McClendons'. He didn't say where he was going, but it was soon obvious that he'd gone to Mrs. Hyatt's house. The town was agog. The Hyatt residence was small. There was an attic loft, people knew, but it was unfinished and uninsulated. It would be a cold place come winter. There were two bedrooms downstairs. There was no guest room. Customers going for fittings inquired discretely how Matty was fitting into the household. The sisters smiled sweetly and said only that it was pleasant to have a man in the house to see to their needs and went on with their work. Matty was seen in constant attendance on Mrs. Hyatt. He attended church with her regularly. Sometimes the seamstress accompanied them, but mostly she seemed content to let them have their privacy. This arrangement prevailed until shortly after Christmas.

In mid-January, on an extremely cold and windy day, there was a knock at Mary McClendon's front door—the door people used when calling on business with the town clerk. Megan answered to find Matty standing huddled in the long greatcoat he'd worn since he first came to town. He wanted to see the town clerk, he informed Megan. When Mary appeared, Megan withdrew as Mary asked what she could do for Matty.

"I want to get a marriage license to marry Mrs. Hyatt," he told her.

Mary wasn't entirely surprised, but she hadn't expected this development so soon—maybe late spring. She gave Matty the necessary papers and helped him fill them out. She inquired politely when the marriage would occur, but Matty seemed not to hear, reluctantly removing three dollars from his leather wallet with the snap top to pay the fee. Taking the license, he left, having said only what was necessary for the transaction.

Mary could hardly wait for his departure before she donned coat and shawl and raced to the store to spread the latest and choicest gossip in years. By the time the noon mail cleared, the town was alerted, but no one knew the date of the nuptials. And they couldn't find out.

The happy couple continued as they had. No one received a wedding invitation. Neither sister nor Matty made mention of the license to a soul. The townspeople were baffled.

Winter tarried long that year. It only grudgingly made way for spring. Matty and Mrs. Hyatt attended church every Sunday, even in severe weather, came out to an occasional church supper, and put in an all-day appearance at town meeting, where Matty was his old self haranguing and arguing the merits of the New Deal and Franklin Roosevelt. Mrs. Hyatt, whose deceased husband had been a very conservative Republican, listened in rapt admiration while Matty expounded his theories. The Democrats fielded their customary slate of candidates, Matty leading the list and running for first selectman. He received twenty-seven votes, his opponent three hundred and ten. The townspeople said that the late Mr. Hyatt must be spinning like a dervish in his grave at the spectacle Mrs. Hyatt had created.

After a long winter, spring burst on the town like a thunderclap. Grass sprang from the soil as if each blade had been a tightly wound helix. Trees and flowers bloomed, sending a blush of fragrance over the town. People emerged from their winter captivity blinking and relieved to be free of their houses.

Matty and Mrs. Hyatt came out each day to walk to the store or to work among the flowers and shrubs, but it seemed that the younger sister joined them more often than she had in the fall. In fact, there were times when Matty and the seamstress walked out alone while Mrs. Hyatt rocked and did needlework on the porch. They still seemed happy, laughing and talking as before, so the neighbors weren't really sure that things had changed.

They weren't sure, that is, until Mrs. Hyatt came down with a severe late spring cold and took to her bed for several days. The seamstress suspended her sewing, telling customers she was sorry but she had to look after her sister. She couldn't be cook, maid, nurse, and seamstress at the same time, she explained. Her customers were understanding and extended their sympathy to Mrs. Hyatt, but they couldn't help notice that the sister and Matty seemed able to find time together, despite having the care of Mrs. Hyatt.

After a week of illness Mrs. Hyatt was up and about, but she did not resume her walks with Matty. Matty now went out with the seamstress every evening. They walked the paths he had walked the previous fall with Mrs. Hyatt, hand-in-hand, very engrossed in each other. There was no doubt now that Matty's attention centered on the seamstress. People wondered and watched.

The summer wore on. Just before Labor Day there was another knock on Mary's front door. Again, Megan greeted Matty, who asked to see Mary on a business matter. When Mary appeared, Matty shifted from foot to foot, very ill at ease.

"Can I help you, Matty?" Mary asked.

Matty took a paper from his inside coat pocket, opened it, and laid it out on the table. It was the marriage license he had purchased the previous fall.

"Well, I come about this license."

"Yes. Do you and Mrs. Hyatt want to get married? Do you want me to marry you?" Mary was sure that a wedding was imminent and could smell a fee for marrying the couple.

Matty shifted uneasily and looked at the carpeting, avoiding eye contact.

"Well, yes. I want to get married, but not to Mrs. Hyatt. We all talked it over, and me and her sister want to get married. I want to exchange this license 'cause it has Mrs. Hyatt's name on it, and get one with her sister's name."

Mary wanted to laugh but covered her mouth. "I don't think I can do that, Matty."

Matty pointed at the license. "It says right on it that the license is good for one year from date of issue. T'aint been but ten months since I bought it, and it ain't been used none. Seems like I should be able to swap it for another. I don't want no cash back or nothin'." Matty had colored just a little and was obviously nettled that such a simple request was being turned down.

But Mary was adamant. "I know the license is valid, Matty, but I can't exchange it. I can issue you another for three dollars. Do you want me to write out another?"

Matty hesitated. He was clearly distressed. He picked up the license, stared at it, pursed his lips, and frowned.

"You sure you can't do no better than that? Don't seem right I should have to buy another license when I got one ain't been used at all." He was almost pleading.

"No, Matty, that's the way it is. I'm sorry. Shall I write another license?" Mary was sympathetic but firm.

Matty weighed the matter some more. Then he sighed.

"No, don't bother. This one's still good. I'll keep it, I guess, and marry Mrs. Hyatt. There ain't three dollars' worth of difference between the two of 'em, anyhow." And with that he stowed the license in the inside pocket of his coat, said good day, and left.

Of course, this development was too good to keep to herself, and Mary quickly spread the word. Everyone chuckled over Matty's dilemma and waited for the wedding. It never did come off. Within days of Matty's second visit to the town clerk, he abruptly left the sisters' residence to move in with Fred Westwood, a bachelor farmer, where he stayed through the next winter.

The sisters never married, although they did take in another boarder, a widower their own age from Orrington. Matty remained single, and the sisters remained mum.

16

EVILS OF THE WEED

The summer days of Maine in June and July were days filled with excitement and freedom. June days, especially, were often cloudless. In the summer of 1937 the sun's rays warmed the earth, turning it into a lush green paradise, a perfect place for an eleven-year-old boy to discover the world and himself. In those months my days were filled with an endless variety of activities. Some, such as the daily tasks Dad set for me in the garden—weeding, hoeing, and harvesting—were chores that I abhorred at first. They were tedious, boring, and backbreaking, but as I matured some of the onus of such chores was leavened by the discovery that the skills I'd developed from being forced to do them were highly marketable.

This discovery resulted in my finding jobs, doing for cash what I did for free at home. Because of the money, I took on these jobs gladly, and the work didn't seem as onerous when performed for others as it was when done for the family. But in time the money I earned from such labors even gilded the tasks at home and I began to take pride in our garden and woodpile.

With my chores and hire-out work, my time for swimming

and play was often limited to afternoons and evenings in the early summer. Of course, there were always days when the whole day could be spent on a fishing trip to Sunrise Farm or on Sunkhaze. On those days Paully, Tommy, and I—and often Louie—would hike to Sunrise Farm about mid-morning with our fishing poles and a lunch to spend the day fishing for blue gills, perch, pickerel, and hornpout.

Dad, to his credit, was tolerant of these fishing trip diversions, often suggesting that I take the day off for one, and even supplying cans of Vienna sausage or deviled ham for lunches. Sometimes he even included Devil Dogs—those scrumptious chocolate and cream-filled cakes made by Drake's Bakery in Rhode Island—and bottles of Sunspot orange soda, all of which I considered gourmet food. I would make thick sandwiches of deviled ham, egg, and mustard on Mama's homemade bread, wrap them in wax paper, and put them in the fish creel. A few fresh cukes, tomatoes, and radishes, along with salt and pepper, went in, too. Fishing always made me hungry.

Tommy's sandwiches weren't as generous and were more likely to be made of sandwich meats on store-bought bread. He also packed Frisbie pies. Louie's sandwiches were almost always identical to mine, but twice the size and number. And Louie always had a sizable piece of freshly baked chocolate cake.

Louie was younger than Tommy and I, but his huge size and phlegmatic disposition made him our physical equal. He lived on a farm with his mother, a cook noted in the community for her pastries. She was used to cooking for her family of six men plus several farm hands, all with prodigious appetites. She always made a double-size lunch for Louie, to be sure her Louie thrived and did not become hungry.

Naturally, with such an abundance of food a great deal of swapping took place at lunchtime. I traded sandwiches with Tommy. He loved the homemade bread that I had, and I loved his store-bought bread. Louie could down a half-dozen cans of Vienna sausage without a burp. His sandwiches—thick slices of white bread with slabs of roast beef or home-cured ham, delighted me. Paully liked

Louie's egg salad-and-olive sandwiches and the Spanish olives and pickles Louie brought. Lunchtime was like a box lunch social, as each of us vied to get his favorite food. Everyone was happy.

Our fishing on these occasions was sporadic. The first hour or two at the bridge over the stream resulted in each of us catching fifteen or twenty fish of various species. They were mostly trash fish, but we saved them all for Dad's pigs. The pigs devoured them with relish—even the blue gills and sunfish with their large, spiny fins.

After lunch, another spate of fishing at Louie's Aunt Violet's camp a short way from the bridge resulted in more fish for the pigs. On very warm days the fish would stop biting by mid-afternoon, and we'd get bored. Boredom is abhorred by young boys in much the same way that nature abhors a vacuum. Ten minutes of boredom would reduce us to a state of nervous energy that was akin to a bomb ticking on a ten-second timer. Boys can't tolerate idleness. It breeds mischief.

When boredom set in, our first resort was swimming—preferably a good stint of skinny-dipping. Off came the tattered shorts and overalls of summer. Clothes were tossed anywhere on the grassy lawn that fronted Aunt Vi's camp above the floating dock, and we cavorted in naked glee before plunging into the water at the end of the float. Water sports could dissipate boredom for at least several hours, but eventually even swimming was tiresome.

Sound carried well along the stream, and our shouts and yells sometimes summoned the teenage daughter of the farm family that lived about a half-mile from Aunt Vi's cottage. Barbie was Louie's cousin and the only child of the Maynards, who owned Sunrise Farm. She was seventeen or eighteen years old, pretty, and quite buxom. We had watched surreptitiously on several occasions when she swam nude, sunning herself languorously and displaying her charms shamelessly for us to ogle. We knew she was aware of our excursions and spying. On the way home after such an afternoon of watching Barbie, we often joked among ourselves that Aunt Vi's cottage was the only place in the world where we could see the "sunrise all day."

But Barbie herself was a Peeping Tom or Tomasina, for she sometimes hid in the bushes and watched us swim. We were quite aware of her eyes on us while we swam and performed all kinds of lewd and acrobatic feats for her benefit. Tommy became quite adept at swimming on his back with only his private appendage protruding from the water. Paully, Louie, and I all jeered at this, yelling out that it would be a great trick if only Tommy had a great prick. Then we dissolved in gales of laughter over our wicked wit.

Sometimes we stopped at Sunrise Farm on our way home and paid our respects to Mrs. Maynard and Barbie. Barbie fawned over us, making arch remarks about the wonderful swimming at Aunt Vi's cottage, while Mrs. Maynard looked perplexed. It all made for a very titillating fishing trip.

But even the excitement that Barbie provided dulled as the summer waned. We emerged from the water after a prolonged swim with our fingers wrinkled and our bodies cold. As we lay about on the lawn in the sun to dry and warm, boredom lay heavy on each of us.

We chatted idly as we were drying. The subject of smoking came up, and we were all struck with the desire to take up the use of tobacco, or "the weed," as the ladies of the Congregational Church Women's Christian Temperance Union called it. Both Dad and Grammy Spruce were fierce enemies of tobacco. Dad was an ex-smoker and had all the righteousness of the sinner saved. Grammy Spruce was equally obsessed with tobacco as the companion and friend of "demon rum."

It was Louie who was the instigator that first time, kindling the fires of hell in the minds of all of us with a sudden desire to taste for ourselves that which had been so vehemently banned. It was late into July, almost into the dog days of August, and the humidity had soared. Louie lay with his head cradled on his bunched-up shirt, idly gazing at his right foot which was crossed over his left. He had found a large and engorged leech on the top of his foot, which we dislodged in the usual manner, by applying a lighted kitchen match to the leech as it dangled from Louie's foot. It sizzled, curled, emitted a puff of steam, and fell off, to everyone's glee. Louie's foot bore a tiny incision from which a bloody rivulet flowed.

"Gawd, I hate bloodsuckers," Louie said with disgust as the leech writhed in the grass. "They're such slippery, slimy things ya can't even catch hold of one when it's stuck itself on ya. I hope ya fry in hell, too, ya slimy son-of-a-bitch!" He spat at the leech, missing it by a wide margin but relieving himself of some of his disgust.

Louie then turned his attention to a patch of weeds nearby with a stand of milkweed and curly dock. The milkweed pods were only just formed and were a long way from being ripe enough to split open with a loud "pop" and spill out their seeds with the long, silky threads, but the curly dock had bloomed early and now proffered long spikes of brown seeds.

"Curly dock is called Indian tobacco because Indians used to smoke it all the time," Louie informed us.

Tommy had been examining his scrotum and penis, both of which had almost shrunk to invisibility. Tommy often complained about the effect of the cold water on his privates. He was proud of them and preferred to have his friends see them at their best.

Forgetting his private parts for a moment, Tommy sneered, "Louie, ya talk like someone with a paper asshole. And you're dumb besides. That stuff on the top of the Indian tobacco is seeds. Ya can't smoke seeds. Dumb-ass!" Tommy liked to swear when we were fishing. It was safe because there were no adults around to hear him.

Louie had been challenged. His intellectual integrity was at stake.

"Ya can too smoke seeds. I done it a couple of times already. And you're the smart-ass. Ya think if ya ain't done something, nobody's done it. Fact is, I smoke a lot. Not just Indian tobacco, either. I smoked half a cigar just the other day. Bet ya haven't done that."

Louie sat up and wet his finger, then wiped some blood from his foot.

"I'm gonna bleed to death from that friggin' bloodsucker. They put stuff in ya that makes your blood thin, ya know."

Tommy had been one-upped, but he didn't retreat. He ignored Louie's concern about impending death from loss of blood and attacked the bigger issue of smoking, which was much more interesting than the leech.

"That's easy to say 'cause nobody saw ya. I bet ya can't smoke any better than the rest of us, and if I had something to smoke I could prove it."

That was a baldfaced dare and a safe one. There probably wasn't a cigar or cigarette within two miles of us.

Louie's face lit up as though bathed by a Klieg light. He had sandbagged Tommy very neatly.

"Ya talk big. Ya think I can't prove I smoked half a cigar. Ya want to smoke? I got some smoke stuff right in my fishbag. I'm gonna see if ya can put ya money where ya mouth is."

Louie got to his feet and lumbered in naked righteousness to his fishbag near the float. He fumbled inside and withdrew a large Edgeworth tobacco can, the kind of can his grandfather bought often at Spruce's Store.

Trotting back to us, he threw the can at Tommy's feet and squatted beside him. Tommy opened the can and poured the contents on the ground. Out fell a small box of matches, a half a cigar, a small bag of Bull Durham cigarette tobacco, and a package of cigarette papers.

"Ya think I was lying? Why would I have all this stuff if I wasn't smoking it? Ya say ya can smoke. Let me make ya a cigarette from that Bull Durham and let's see ya smoke. Smart-ass!"

Before Tommy could protest, Louie pulled a paper from the pack, held it inexpertly between thumb and forefinger of his left hand, and sprinkled some tobacco from the bag. He shook the paper to level the load, then rolled it into a lumpy cylinder, licked the edge of the paper, and produced a very damp and dubious appearing cigarette. He handed his creation to Tommy.

"Think ya can light it up by yourself?" he challenged.

Tommy eyed the cigarette.

"You said ya smoked a cigar. Ya didn't say anything about this kind of stuff."

Louie jeered. "Ya, I knew you'd chicken out. I said Indian tobacco was smoked by Indians. Ya said you could smoke it, too. I'm giving ya better stuff to prove you're not chicken. I ain't gonna give away my cigar to someone don't know how to smoke. Now are ya chicken or not, smart-ass?"

Tommy paled and looked a little sick, but he had to meet the challenge. He stuck the cigarette between his lips, very gingerly, fat end first. He selected a match from the box and scratched it. The match flared, startling him, but he quickly recovered and leaned towards the flame. His judgment was bad and the flame missed the cigarette and singed the long lock of blond hair that always hung low over Tommy's right eye. The hair charred in the flame and a whisp of smoke ascended skyward along with the stench of burning hair.

Tommy was game, ignored the stench and his burned hair, and took another stab at the flame, jerking his head to connect flame to cigarette. The twisted paper end erupted in a bright yellow flame which flared up to char the remaining strands of his seared hair, giving him a completely new hairstyle.

Tommy took a long drag. It was a serious mistake. He belched smoke, coughing violently while his eyes teared copiously. Louie was gleeful.

"Ya see! Ain't as easy as ya think. Gimme that butt and I'll show ya how it's done." He grabbed the cigarette.

Tommy folded. Still gasping, he forfeited the butt and Louie took a long, expert drag, held the smoke in his lungs, then exhaled with a loud sigh. He exclaimed triumphantly, "That's how it's done. Smart-ass! And ya don't move ya head toward the match, ya dummy. Ya move the match to the cigarette. Ya look like ya stuck ya head in a furnace."

Then he turned to me. "Ya want to dry a drag? Just a little one. Be careful. Don't inhale. Here, try it!" He thrust the butt at me.

I didn't really want to try it, but the pressure was too great. With the butt gingerly pinched between thumb and forefinger, I took a puff. This time the cigarette flared again into a bright glow. I felt heat under my eyes before I tasted the acrid bitter smoke. I sucked too hard and smoke went down my throat. It entered my lungs, rich Kentucky burley, and choked me. At the same time I felt my head explode. I was very lightheaded and the grass blurred. I coughed and exhaled. Some of the smoke escaped through my nose, burning the membranes and smarting my eyes. Despite the pain I mumbled, "Tastes pretty good," and managed a sickly smile while I stifled another cough.

Louie took another drag after he retrieved the butt from me, then handed it to Tommy. This time Tommy succeeded in taking a tiny puff and blowing out smoke without coughing. He had taken the butt as if it were a delightful piece of manna offered by some beautiful goddess—or maybe Barbie Big Boobs—while actually thinking that the hateful, stinking thing had come directly from hell, reeking of brimstone and delivered by the devil incarnate. But the wages of sin are the pleasures of the flesh and the corruption of the soul, and this drag, carefully taken, was tolerable. Perhaps he could master this new and debauched pastime and enjoy it with his other vices, swearing and occasional masturbation.

The cigarette didn't last long. Louie went over to the nearest dock plant and stripped some of the seed tassels. He carefully rolled another cigarette, this time into a neat cylinder. Applying another match, Louie deftly lit the new butt. It glowed red and aromatic. The smoke smelled better than the tobacco, rich and heady like the sandalwood incense that Mama sometimes burned after she cooked cabbage. Louie and Tommy each tried a few puffs, but it was hard to keep the stuff lit. The glow died away between drags.

"Damn stuff's too green," Louie opined. "It needs to set in the sun for a day to cure. Don't want it too dry, though—flames up then." We all listened to Louie with new reverence. He really did have some expertise in the art of smoking.

Paully wanted to try, but I wouldn't let him. He was still too young for vice. It was okay to sit around nude and go skinny-dipping and swear a little, but real sinning was something for Paully's future. I secretly hoped that Paully would do most of his sinning on his own. I didn't want to know about it.

We finished off the rest of Louie's meager supply of Bull Durham and the half cigar. Gradually the slight dizziness that accompanied each drag abated, and I slowly attained some skill in inhaling cigarette smoke. But the cigar was different. It was too strong and rancorous to inhale.

"Ya not supposed to inhale a seegar," Louie said. "Ya supposed to hold the smoke in ya mouth, sort of, and enjoy the taste. A good cigar is like a good woman. They are made to be enjoyed by men." Louie blew a cloud of cigar smoke that, if it had been a woman, could never have been called a "good woman." The cigar was far too cheap to have produced anything but a tart.

Tommy couldn't let Louie's sophistry go unchallenged.

"What da ya know about women, anyhow? Just cause ya can smoke a cigar don't mean ya know nothing about women. Besides, with that dinky little thing of yours, ya better stick to smoking. Ya chances are better."

The conversation turned to women but ended with the last drag on the cigarette. The fishing trip had been a memorable one, providing a new vice for us to enjoy.

But that first attempt at smoking didn't go unnoticed or unpunished. That night at supper Dad was asking about how the fishing trip went when he suddenly leaned close to me and said, "Look up at me. Have you been smoking?"

The blood drained from my entire body into the soles of my feet. I obeyed all my natural instincts. I lied baldly, badly, and adamantly.

Dad knew I was lying. He always did. It was uncanny how he could spot lying. This time Dad was aided and abetted by my total lack of eyelashes, burned away by that first searing drag on the devil's coffin nail. The interrogation was relentless.

"Where did you get the cigarettes? What about the matches? Who was with you? How many cigarettes did you smoke? Just one? Don't tell me you smoked just one. Your eyebrows and eyelashes look like you had your head in the furnace! I can see your hair is singed, too. Did Tommy and Louie smoke?"

I squealed on both my friends. I sang like a nightingale. I blurted out everything. I threw myself on Dads mercy, but he offered not a twinge of it. He thundered about the dangers of smoking, his rage feeding on his words and turning him into an inferno of fiery verbiage. I could only cringe at his scathing attack, which ended with this dire warning:

"Do you want to stunt your growth? Haven't I told you that smoking causes TB and you know your Uncle Millard died of TB? You're lucky this time, but if I ever hear of you smoking again, you're going to sit here and smoke a whole pack of Camels right in front of your mother. And in front of Grammy Spruce, too!"

I looked properly repentant and ashamed at the threat. Smoking in front of Mama just didn't seem too bad, but I wasn't sure I was ready for a whole pack of Camels. Smoking a whole pack of Camels right in Grammy's face was just too shameful. Grammy Spruce was an ardent member of the WCTU, and she had "spells" which caused her to faint unexpectedly. I would face Beelzebub himself to avoid a confrontation with my grandmother. I prostrated myself cravenly, begging for anything but that. Dad in his majesty was merciful, and I had to do the dishes that night while my sisters leered and made puffing sounds with their pursed lips.

The next morning I learned that Tommy had also been discovered. His mother had spotted his charred locks of hair, and his father—an inveterate smoker of Camel cigarettes—had lectured him severely on the evils of smoking. Tommy's penance was to clean up the dank, dark cellar, removing all the trash. I hope God remembers that I helped him do a good job of it.

The evil lure of the weed was too enticing to put aside simply because it was forbidden, however. We took up the art of smoking in earnest, determined to become proficient in the underworld of forbidden smokers. We had learned an important lesson in our first attempt. Smoking is bad for your health, but only if you get caught.

We learned to light up without singing our hair or eyelashes.

Chewing a mouthful of tender chives or onion tops from the garden hid any tobacco breath. But tobacco wasn't what we smoked most. We discovered lettuce and endive cigarettes. These vegetables grew in abundance in our gardens, and when dried and cured made an acceptable smoke, milder and certainly cheaper than tobacco.

Our search for new and better smokes was the result of having smoked up all the Indian tobacco in the neighborhood. We tried other things, among them crushed oak and maple leave, shredded pine needles, corn silk, and hay chaff, all of which were dangerously flammable and burst into flame with every inhalation. We kept looking for a tobacco substitute to satisfy our cravings—we were smoking junkies hooked not on the weed, but on the exhilaration of the forbidden.

So Tommy and I embarked on a program of curing our own smokes by picking quantities of the plants and drying them in the sun on the shed roof, where we thought they'd be safe from any discovery. Lettuce and endive each offered a rather mild smoke that was easy to inhale and didn't make us dizzy like tobacco sometimes did.

Our curing operation was going along nicely until Mama noticed the pans of drying lettuce on the roof while she was hanging clothes out to dry. Her inquiries nearly caused me to panic, but I rose to the occasion and instantly concocted a story about drying parsley and other garden herbs for her use in the winter when she made those delicious soups and stews. Mama was easy to con. She believed my story and was pleased that I was so thoughtful.

Cigarette paper also proved easy to obtain. Mama kept a supply of tissue paper for gift wrapping that worked well, although it burned faster than real papers. But this problem was moot when we discovered that we could make our own corncob pipes quite easily from the larger ears of sweet corn, stolen from the garden. These lent a certain rakishness to the smoking that plain cigarettes never offered. I fancied myself as Tom Sawyer or Huck Finn as I smoked up my latest craze in tobacco substitutes while Tommy prated on about the merits of lettuce versus escarole or Bull Durham.

August passed in a cloud of smoke that year. Several times a week we retired to the depths of the woods by the railroad tracks to smoke up a storm with our pipes and lettuce leaf tobacco. Our favorite smoking place remained Aunt Vi's cottage beside the pond, where we could lie naked in the sun, puffing studiously away while we reflected on the sheer joy of life and what Barbie's breasts might actually feel like. Tommy even learned to blow smoke rings, something I could not master.

But like all vices, constant indulgence in the vice dulls the appetite, summer was rapidly ending, and soon we were concentrating on school clothes, notebooks, pens, and pencils. But the fishing trips had taught us all a lot that summer. I was dubious that future summers would ever be the equal of the one just gone. I was right. My boyhood went up with the smoke of the summer of sin, and the following year I had no time for such foolishness. I discovered girls.

17

No Place to Spit

I loved going to school. There was something exciting every day in learning about the world and the people of the world. I didn't mind the tasks of reading lessons in history, geography, English language, and literature. The lessons didn't seem like tasks—they were labors of love. Recitation periods under the direction of Mr. Billings were exciting times when Mr. Billings, who seemed to know so much about the world, fired my imagination with talk of distant places, historical times, and the heroes of history and literature. Mr. Billings was a wonderful storyteller, bringing to life whatever subject he taught. Even math was fun when Mr. Billings taught it.

But not even Mr. Billings' creative teaching could entirely keep at bay the ennui of an endless Maine winter. By mid-February or early March cabin fever wasn't just rampant in the homes of Milford; it took its toll on us schoolchildren, too. Lincoln's birthday and Washington's birthday offered a brief respite with special exercises and assemblies in commemoration of the great men. Valentine's Day was celebrated with a valentine box in every classroom and an afternoon valentine party with ice cream and cookies from the school board, but these events only served to delay our total descent into apathy by the end of February.

The winter I was in seventh grade had seen a particularly long and snowy one. In early March snow was still three feet deep on the lawns, and the weather was still bitter. The February thaw had come late and was short-lived. March came in like a lion, maddened and raging, as if its kill had been stolen. People hunkered down and hungered for spring.

Finally, in the second week of March, it warmed suddenly. The temperature shot up from the teens at noontime to the mid-forties. Hearts beat faster and spirits soared as temperatures rose to the fifties on the third day of the first March thaw. That day it reached fifty-five by noon, and we went home to dinner exuberant in newly found excitement. Spring was just around the corner. The air was latent with the promise of pussy willows and green grass to come.

As we returned to school after our noonday meal, no one hurried inside the classroom that day. Instead, we gathered on the south side of the school building to stand in the sun. The foundation of the building had a ledge that went entirely around the building. It was twelve to eighteen inches high and wide, and made a perfect place to idle. The snow there had melted, and the concrete had actually warmed enough to be an enticing place to sit. It was crowded with children when I got back to school after dinner.

In the midst of the many, I found my cronies. They were gathered, as usual, in their own group and Hobart Libby was the center of attention. This wasn't unusual, because Hobart had extremely poor eyesight and was often the butt of sometimes mean jokes. Today, however, Hobie had become the envy of the group.

With his head thrown back so that he could see better through his thick glasses, he was demonstrating a newly acquired skill to his circle of friends. Hobie's cheeks were those of a chipmunk in a hazelnut patch. The left cheek was rounded and puffed, while the right cheek, although somewhat smaller, seemed to be masticating. As I approached for a closer look, Hobie's mouth pursed and a brownish stream arched into the air to land in a foul splat in the dirty snow at my feet. My astonishment brought forth jeers.

"Look out for Hobie, Franny. He's loaded."

"Hobie's got a wad to choke a horse. He can spit ten feet upwind."

"He can't see for shit, but boy can he spit!"

I backed away, because Hobie's face was writhing like a gunnysack full of half-grown kittens and I expected another deluge to come hurtling my way at any moment. Being spit upon was bad enough, but a mouthful of vile tobacco juice was disgusting.

At a safe distance, my disgust turned to curiosity. I saw that while Hobie had the largest wad of tobacco in his mouth, other mouths were busy working up their own chews. Furthermore, Hobie was the supplier of these wads. He held half an Apple Cut Plug in his right hand and a jackknife in the other. Ejecting another brown stream in my direction, he asked, "Want a chew? Or are you too chicken?"

I had learned to smoke that past summer, but it wasn't something I did much now. Winter wasn't a season that lent itself to debaucheries such as smoking, and the novelty of that new vice had worn off with the greater excitement of school.

But a charge of being chicken couldn't go unchallenged. All faces turned towards me as Hobie sawed off a sizable cut of the tarry-looking plug and passed it over to me. I accepted it as if I'd been handed a red hot brick. It was horrid looking stuff, evil smelling, and probably vile tasting, but I took it with what I hoped would seem eager anticipation. With as much braggadocio as I could muster, I stuffed my mouth and started to chew. The taste wasn't too bad, but it was bitter and strong and I didn't like the texture.

"Some of us are gonna chew in school. It'll make all the girls sick to see us. You wanna try it, too?" It was another veiled dare, and I nodded with dumb acquiescence and spat my first juice. Most of it ran down my chin. I wiped it off with my hand and wiped my hand on my pants. I'd better practice spitting hard and fast. It was almost time for the bell.

The bell rang and we lined up to march into the school. Hobie pocketed his wad and the rest of us followed suit. The first period that afternoon was a seventh grade study period for the history lesson that was to come. Mr. Billings had eighth grade recitation during that time and was on the eighth grade side of the room.

Shortly after classes began, Hobie retrieved his wad from his pocket and stuffed it in his mouth. The dare had been laid on again. One by one each of us aped Hobie until every mouth had its charge, all of the wads in the left cheek. From the right hand of the room where Mr. Billings stood near the bank of windows, it would be hard to see the bulging cheeks.

Study time allowed students to visit with one another as long as quiet prevailed. Phyllis Frazer, who sat alone at a desk separated from the rest of her row by the four-foot-wide hot-air register, was the focus of many visits. Her sudden popularity nearly overwhelmed her, since she wasn't a popular girl, being considered too bright and a teacher's pet. But Phyllis's visitors didn't linger at her desk. Each boy appeared at her right side, spit a copious quantity of tobacco juice surreptitiously into the floor register, and returned to his desk to generate more juice for the next trip. Phyllis was soon paling visibly with each new visitor.

Her unwelcome popularity came to an end after about ten minutes of profound expectoration when Mr. Billings announced in the stentorian tones he affected for disciplinarian purposes, "You people in seventh grade. No more visiting. And all you fellows with something in your mouth—keep it there until this period is over."

Mr. Billings began edging his way towards the seventh graders. Every one of us with a wad of tobacco in his mouth knew that the game was up. We waited for the coup de grâce.

But the axe didn't fall. Rather, Mr. Billings completed the recitation period for the eighth grade from his new position close to the seventh grade. Then he turned to his next class, now consisting of numerous boys with mouths that were rapidly filling with tobacco juice that was threatening to drown them in their own spit. And to an almost equal number of wide-eyed girls, all trying in vain not to titter at our discomfort.

Mr. Billings' opening remarks ignored the boys as he called on several girls. Each of the girls would have normally avoided recitation, but today each reveled in her role of assistant torturer. My tobacco was growing like Topsy in my mouth. I couldn't believe the volume of saliva I was generating. I sought desperately for a place to spit, but the register was twenty feet away. There was no place to spit. I was obliged to swallow. My Adam's apple bobbed, and down went juice. My only solace was the pain I saw on the faces of my friends.

Willie Mack was the first to go. His face drained of color, Willie raised a hand. Mr. Billings nodded in Willie's direction.

"Permission to go to the basement?" Willie gasped. Mr. Billings nodded, and Willie rose and fled.

In five more minutes it was a total rout, as one after another of us begged for permission to go to the basement. I held on to the end, hoping desperately that Mr. Billings would turn his back just long enough for me to remove that hateful wad that was strangling me, but Mr. Billings was relentless in his scrutiny, and there was still no place to spit. I was forced to beg, too, and joined the others just in time to vomit my dinner into the urinal.

Some of the boys who had been sick first were already recovering a little, although they were still green and wan when I joined them. Some of us were still groaning and retching when Mr. Billings made his appearance. He looked at us in utter disgust.

"You boys are lucky I didn't make you keep that stuff in your mouths until you all died, but I hope you learned something from this. I won't keep you after school. You have all had enough, I guess. You'd better go home now so you'll feel better tomorrow. I don't ever want to see chewing tobacco in my school again." He strode out with the dignity of an emperor.

We left one by one as our strength returned. I was prostrate for half an hour before I could walk slowly home. Mama was surprised to see me home from school at three o'clock, but her surprise turned to concern when she saw that I wasn't feeling good. She had me lie on the couch in the kitchen and offered to give me some hot tea.

The thought of it almost made me retch again.

My siblings came home at their regular time, and I was relieved that none of them seemed aware that anything unusual had happened at school. By five I was feeling well enough to do the chores. The woodboxes got special attention because I had premonitions of impending doom, and a little extra attention to my chores might stand me in good stead.

At supper time I was feeling well enough to eat a small supper. Mama asked, "Would you like me to make you an egg on toast?" but Dad didn't seem to hear her question and didn't ask why I couldn't eat what the others were eating.

There were canned peaches for dessert. They were one of my favorites, and as I spooned up my first bite, I heard Dad ask, a little too casually, "Anything special happen at school today?"

I froze, a spoonful of canned peaches halfway to my mouth. Cold fear chased up my spine while I waited for Ellen or Paul to answer.

Ellen said, "Joan Violette peed her pants again and it ran under Miss Weeks's desk and Miss Weeks put sawdust on it from the box she keeps in the closet for when Joan pees on the floor."

Paul was impressed and tried to one-up Ellen. "Willie Bond pooped right out loud when we was reading. And Mrs. MacDonald said we didn't need any unnecessary noises during reading class. And Willy said it wasn't an unnecessary noise. It was a fart. He doesn't know you're not supposed to say fart in school, I guess."

Mama looked at Paul sternly and said, "We don't say that word at the table, Paully. Even if Willie did say it in school. It's not a nice word."

But Paully had the last word, because he retorted, "But that's what he said, and Dad wanted to know if something unusual happened in school." Paully always told the truth.

Dad came to Paully's aid. "It's all right, Paully. But just say 'poop' from now on, so Mama will be happy." Then Dad turned to me and said with great concern, "I understand you've taken up a new habit, Franny. Mr. Billings was telling me that he's glad that you never chew gum in school, but that he's afraid that he can't let you chew tobacco, either."

Then Dad went on. "Do you chew any special brand of tobacco, 'cause I brought home some Apple Cut Plug for you this evening. That's what most men chew. We sell more of that than anything. Hobie Libby's grandfather chews that all the time. If Hobie was to chew, I expect he'd chew Apple, too." Dad reached into his pocket and withdrew a half plug of Apple and laid it beside my plate.

"There, that's enough for this evening. I'll just cut off a good chew for you." Dad reached for his jackknife.

I almost lost my supper as the thought of the tobacco I'd chewed that afternoon brought back the nausea. All eyes were on me. I was trapped. I'd have to chew more of the horrible stuff.

"No, no, I don't want to ever chew that stuff again. I only did it 'cause the others did and they dared me. I don't want to get sick again." I implored Dad to forgive me.

Dad seemed undecided. "Well, I don't want you to feel like you've got to sneak around to chew, but if you really don't want some tonight, I guess I'll just have to take this back to the store. But I think you'd better do up all the dishes by yourself tonight. That will probably help keep your mind off chewing tobacco."

I usually listened to Scattergood Baines right after supper, but missing Scattergood on the radio was a lot better than getting sick again. Dad put the Apple plug back in his pocket, and the girls grinned at being freed of their chores at my expense.

Mama and Paully were sympathetic, though. Mama made excuses to linger in the kitchen, scraping pots and cleaning the table while I did the dishes. Paully hovered around and put the pots away to show his sympathy.

"I'm glad you aren't going to chew tobacco," Paully said. "It's an awful hard thing to do when you're in the house, and it can make you feel awful bad and awful sick, especially when you've got no place to spit." Paully always told the truth.

18

THAT'S NOT THE ROAD

Dad occasionally hired Baptiste Michaud (pronounced Bar-teest Mee-show) to yard his firewood from the cutting place to a field where it could easily be hauled home by Dad's brother Ray in his truck. Yarding wood was a task I always enjoyed, no matter who I worked with, and Baptiste was a colorful teamster.

My first encounter with Baptiste was during winter vacation on a February day in 1938, when Dad dropped me off at Third Stream Bridge where Baptiste was already waiting with his team and sled. He was a wisp of a man, wearing a red plaid hunter's cap with earflaps down and a matching mackinaw. He had several days' growth of gray beard and a mouthful of yellow fangs. He spoke Franglais, my term for his fractured English. Dad introduced me to Baptiste in French. Baptiste nodded several times with lots of smiles, then turned to me and shook hands.

"Me. I, Baptiste Michaud, am wan happy man, me. To have young boy like you for to help me is good. We make good team, us. We bring you papa's wood to field and have fun, too. You papa say you very good boy and work hard. I see you got big lunch for to eat.

Big lunch is veree good. Me, when I work big, I eat big, too, me. I t'ink big boy like you eat big alla time, no?" Baptiste seemed to approve of me as a helper, and I liked him immediately, although his fractured English was a little hard to follow, since he spoke in a high voice and very rapidly. But the day was starting well.

After Dad gave Baptiste some instructions in French as to where his wood was to be piled, Dad left, saying I could ride into town with Baptiste at the end of the day. And we were off to the cutting grounds. There was a lot of snow, over a foot, and the horses had to break trail the first trip in. The road was plain to see in the chopping area, but once there I would have to show Baptiste where we had stacked our wood. There were about twenty cords in all, scattered over the chopping, but I knew exactly where each pile was because I had piled most of them myself.

It was a good five hundred yards from the County Road across an abandoned hayfield to the stream, which was well frozen over, much to Baptiste's delight. Nevertheless, he stopped to inspect the ice and crossing, all the time talking loudly to himself and to me.

"Thees hice. It preety hard, him. I t'ink Bob and Jeem be hokay here. Not break trew de hice. Mebbe de hice he crack, him, but is good when hice crack and pack down hard on bottom of stream. I like dat. Bime by we know for sure whan we come back with first load." Satisfied that the ice was safe and that the brook would not be a problem, we climbed back on the sled and Baptiste gave the reins a slap to get Bob and Jim moving.

It was uphill for nearly a quarter of a mile to the chopping. The road was several years old and well defined. There was a tendency for the sled to slide sideways as the road slanted to our right. This caused some concern to Baptiste, who remarked, "The sled, she's slide to right. Mebbe whan we come back with wood the sled slide too much. But we got lots of snow, us, so mebbe we hokay. I t'ink is gonna be warm day and snow get sticky. We try to make good track."

At the top of the hill we entered the woods, and I pointed out the tote road Dad and I had swamped out earlier in the winter. It looked different now, narrower than I remembered and much less smooth, although the heavy snow had rounded and softened all the dips and humps. Baptiste turned the horses down the road and they put their shoulders into the traces, plodding along, breaking trail in earnest now.

"This road goes straight on for a bit then makes a big loop where we've made our piles of wood. It comes back on itself, so we can come out easy," I told Baptiste.

He nodded and grinned, showing his broken yellow teeth. "Hokay we go for end of loop. Load up coming back. Bob and Jeem like dat better. Mebbe we go all ze way around first time to make good track for sled. Dan we load hup good." He drummed the reins on the horses' backs again and they heaved the sled forward. We made the circle in about fifteen minutes, by which time the horses had heated up and their backs and flanks were steaming. The sun was getting high, and it felt warm on us already.

On the second trip up the loop our sled widened the first track and packed the snow into a nice rut. Once the sled was loaded, the horses would have it easy back to the field, for it was mostly down-hill and excellent sledding. Baptiste was delighted with the prospects for the day and kept up a constant chatter.

"You papa, he's gonna be happee tonight, him. We gonna do wan big work, us. You see. Baptist Michaud is good woodman, me." We stopped beside the furthermost pile from the yard.

There was a broom behind the sled seat that Baptiste handed to me. "Franee, you be big sweeper. Sweep off snow on pile so we load wood more easy, us. I take big piss here to mark where we start. Last night I drink much beer. This morneeng, Baptiste is big pisser, but is good for belly." Baptiste urinated by the horses and I cleared the snow.

Things went well right from the first. Baptiste was small but agile and very strong for his size. Our wood was mostly white birch and maple, with some oak and some yellow birch. The four-foot sticks were cut from trees six to twelve or fourteen inches in diameter on average. They were frozen solid, and our wood hooks hardly dented the ends of the logs, but Baptiste heaved his wood onto the sled like he was lifting toothpicks. Of course there were smaller logs in the pile, too, but it was all heavy work. I was twelve at the time and had handled a lot of wood before, so I was no novice. But I had to hustle to keep up with Baptiste. It wasn't long before we were both sweating as much as the horses. I stopped to take off my outer jacket, and Baptiste turned to me.

"You papa say you veree fine worker. He say right to me, him. But we doan got to rush too much, us. We got long day. Is much better we go just right fast so we not get too hot and tired. That way we do more steady and yard more wood. Hokay?"

We had put on nearly two cord when Baptiste declared it enough for the first load. I was really warm, and the prospect of a rest sounded good. We climbed on the sled and Baptiste whipped up the horses.

"H'yo boys. Time to pull hard. Make Baptiste proud to have good horses like you. H'yo!" He gave another slap with the reins, the horses lurched into their harness, and the sled jerked forward. We were off with the first load.

It was my first time yarding, and I was a little nervous. We went slowly around the loop and out onto the short turn-off road. At the main road Baptiste pulled up on the reins.

"Whoa, whoa, back. Halt you big bastards! We rest before we go fast down the hill."

Baptiste said "basTARDS" instead of "BAStards," but the word was a term of endearment to him. He loved those horses. The strain of the first heavy pulling must have affected the horses, for now they both lifted their tails and deposited piles of dung in the track. Then they urinated profusely, which seemed to remind Baptiste that he, too, needed to go.

"Men and horses who work big, make good pissers. Veree healthy to piss good."

After several minutes Baptiste got back on the sled, whipped up the reins again, and said, "H'yo, here we go down the hill." The horses leaned into the traces and off we went, Baptiste standing straight up on the sled bed and pulling back strongly on the reins. It was a wild ride down the hill. The snow was soft and wet enough to be very fast for the sled. The horses didn't need to pull at all. They had to push back to keep the sled from overtaking them. Baptiste pulled and yelled, "Easee, easee! Hold it, boys. Not go fast. Easee, there!"

The sled wanted to slide to the left as we went down the hill, and Baptiste had to keep the horses from yawing to the right. The sled crabbed left over and over. I hung on for dear life, all the time thinking the load was going to spill off.

At the halfway point where the hill flattened, the sled came straight and we went into the final pitch straight down. There was no sliding here. The horses took to their heels and we fairly flew down the slope and onto the flat at the brook. Baptiste whipped them up as we pounded across the ice and started up the opposite bank.

"Pull, you basTARDS, PULL! YOU STOP NOW, I, BAP-TISTE MICHAUD, KILL YOU ALL DEAD! Go-go-go-go!" And then we were on the field. The horses slowed down on their own, and I could see that they knew exactly what they were doing. We stopped. Baptiste peeled off his hat and swung it in a circle.

"By Gawd, that wan good ride. Bob and Jeem veree fine hors-es, them. I tell you someting, Franee. You gran'papa, he show me to be teamster. Dat long time before. Mebbe 1910 or 1912. I come from Rivière-du-Loup. A young man, me. Joe Pelletier, he hire me cut wood with him, and he teach me how to drive horses. My papa had no horse in Cana-Da. Only hox. Hox strong, but slow and dumb. Not like good horse. Horse smart, quick. Strong, too. I want to buy horse, and bime-by I do. You have good gran'papa. I t'ank him many times, me. Now we go to edge of field and unload first load. H'yo!" And we did just that.

The rest of the day was gorgeous. With each load, the road got better. By noon the snow was melting in our ruts and the bare earth showed on the hill. That was good. It slowed our sled and made it easier for the horses on the downgrade. We made three more trips before noon, getting out almost eight cords. Dad was waiting for us on the fourth trip with my lunch. Mama had given me my favorite sandwiches—thick slabs of baloney laid in her homemade white bread, and a thermos of hot tea.

Baptiste pulled a beatup agate-ware dinner bucket from under the seat of the sled and opened it to exclaim over his lunch of biscuits filled with "cauteau," a French-Canadian sausage meat made from pork. After putting nose bags full of oats on the horses, we all ate. Then Dad scaled out his pile.

"At this rate you guys will get it all yarded easily by tomorrow, for sure. That's great!"

Baptiste beamed. "Emile. You boy, Franee, here. He wan good sledman, him. Good as big man. Work hard. I tell him how you papa learn me to drive horse twenty year ago. I t'ink Joe also learn Franee some t'ings, him. Franee say he go with you papa to woodlot many times. Is good whan papas teach boys to work."

Dad was proud as punch at Baptiste's praise of my work. He went back to work at the store all smiles and happy. We went back to our yarding tasks. The afternoon was pure fun. Baptiste was a great storyteller, and he told me of a recent encounter he'd had with Lin Jordan. Lin had tried to hire Baptiste and his team to yard some pine logs in back of Bradley. Baptiste needed the work, he explained, but he didn't want to work for the money Lin was offering. When Baptiste reported to Lin's office on Water Street in Old Town, he had been offered ten dollars a day to yard the logs.

"Lin Jordan, he sit in his big chair in hoffice, him, and he say, 'I pay you ten dollars a day to yard pine logs to Great Works Stream. Is easy yard. Plenty good snow. What you say, Baptiste? You yard for me, yes?'

"Lin, he sit behind big desk, him. He wear fine suit to work. I t'ink he t'ink I am wan dumb Frenchman, me. So I say to him, 'You give me helpair to roll logs on skids?'

"Lin, he look at me and say, 'Yes, but you pay him $3,20 a day from what I pay you.' Now I know he t'ink I am dumb Frenchman from Cana-Da who drink too much Pickswick Ale, so I look him in the eye and all I say is laugh, me. Then I say, 'Au revoir,' and walk hout.

"Four days later, he send for me. I am talking with men in his mill to find hout why Lin is looking for other mans to yard his logs. Not his mill mens. Thay all say, 'Oh, is lots of snow and haul is not long, but it over small cranberry bog and veree bad for horses.' I say to me, 'Aha! Now I knows why he calls Baptiste.' So I go back to see him and he is still hasking me to yard his logs.

"This time he say to me, 'Hokay, I send one of my mens with you, and I pay him.' He t'ink I jump for him, now. But I look him in eye and I say, 'Veree good. But I find hout about big bog I have to cross. Bogs is very bad for my horses. I yard your logs for twelve dollars and that my final price.' He lookat me real long time, then he say, "Hokay, I should have taken your first offer. Next time I will. Start tomorrow on logs.' It was good job. I work two weeks. Make good money, me, and from Lin Jordan, too! I still say laugh when I t'ink of it."

I laughed, too, at Baptiste's story. It wasn't often that anyone got the better of Jordan, I had learned, but some did. And I later found out that those who did were the very people he hired over again. Perhaps he had his own formula for getting really good help.

On our second load that afternoon, we were nearly unloaded when a car drew up and stopped. A man dressed in fancy hunting clothes got out and came over to us.

"I'm looking for the Haines Ridge Road. How much farther is it?"

Baptiste threw a big birch log onto the pile and turned to the man. "Oh, long way from here. Mebbe six-seven mile, him."

"Can you tell me how to find it?" the man queried.

"Sure t'ing. I work in dat place many times, me. About a mile and half from here, you come to big hill. Dat Baker Brook Hill. You go down hill, cross bridge, and you see little road on right. Dat not it!

"Now you go some more, mebbe half-mile, come to other road on right. Much bigger road. You see it good. Dat not it, either. You go past dat road mebbe another mile, you come around big turn and see some more good road on right and veree bad roads on left.

Dose roads not it, either." Each time Baptiste had described a road, the man had expected it to be the Haines Ridge Road, and now he was looking puzzled. Baptiste, however, continued his instructions.

"Next you come to Little Birch Stream Bridge. A good road on left. It go into woods alongside stream, but dat not road. Half-mile farther, you cross Big Birch Stream. This is big stream with falls. Just before bridge is good road on right and just after bridge is good road on left. Don't go on dese roads. They not the ones. Go mebbe two miles and you see no roads in that two miles. Dan you go up small hill where road is veree wide, him. At top of hill is big wide spot in road and small road on right, not veree good to find. Dat's it. Dat's Haines Ridge Road. Is easy to find from here. You remember how I tell you where is road?" Baptiste was delighted to have helped. The man was looking perplexed.

"I'm not sure I got all that," he said to me.

I said, "Oh, it's easy to find. It's the first road on the right after you pass Little and Big Birch Streams. It's not used much anymore, but the road and clearing are wide because so many park there to hunt. Are you going to hunt? It's good rabbit country." He didn't look like a hunter, even though he was dressed like one.

"No," he replied. "I'm on my way to Crocker Turn Camps. My father once cut wood in that area, and I was just curious as to where it is. Thanks for the directions." He drove off.

I never knew whether he found the road, but I'm sure he recalls the directions—or the non-directions—that Baptiste gave him.

We did one more trip that afternoon and quit early, leaving a short day's work for the next day. The three miles back to town were pleasant—more stories from Baptiste about his days in the woods. We drove up in front of the store about five. Baptiste went inside with me. The mail crowd was there, and everyone knew Baptiste. He kind of strutted like a bantam rooster, letting jibes roll off him good-naturedly. He proclaimed me a great sledman and helper. Dad came out of the meat room with two quarts of Pickwick Ale, which he gave to Baptiste, saying, "Be sure to go back tomorrow. If you don't

I'll take the price of your ale off your pay."

The next day we finished the yarding easily. I worked with Baptiste several times after that, and not always when he was working for Dad. That he hired me to work with him for others, I always considered a compliment. And he paid me four dollars a day, to boot.

19

FERGUS'S FARTING HORSES

Fergus Fenney was a farmer in Sunkhaze who delighted in telling tall stories and thinking up outrageous practical jokes. He was a tall man, as thin as a cattail reed, with exceedingly long arms and legs. His face resembled the feed bag of one of his horses, weathered and creased from the bitter cold of long, Maine winters, and the hot, steamy field work of Maine summers. He dressed like a farmer, in blue denim shirts and bib overalls, and in winter his gum rubber boots were often caked with manure from the barn and his clothing reeked with the aromas of his animals. He made no apologies for his aura. Once or twice, when he was asked to sit upwind from some more fastidious man around the stove at the store, he replied heatedly that, "They's nothin' wrong 'bout the smell of good, honest hoss or cow shit. If I had to change clothes every time I went in and out of my barn, I'd never git no work done."

One topic Fergus never tired of discussing was horses. Fergus was truly proud of his horseflesh, deeming himself to have a keen eye for good horses. He had owned a pair of mares for a long time that he greatly favored, but they were getting old and no longer gave him bragging rights at the pulling contests. He decided it was time to trade horses. A trip to Veazie was in order.

Barney Gass was a cattle and horse dealer in Veazie, and also owned a sizable automobile junkyard. He had a pair of beautifully matched geldings, young and untrained, and they had caught Fergus's eye. They had no galls, had excellent teeth, and were broken to harness. It was obvious that they had never been worked in the woods. They were expensive, but Fergus would have them. He loved a good trade, and trading horses was the biggest challenge of all.

Barney himself was no slouch at a trade. That's how he made his living. But Fergus had come prepared. He had his mares and his wife's recently purchased used Nash, from which he hoped to raise extra cash. Fergus and Barney dickered, insulting each other often, each going for the jugular, but in the end Fergus had his geldings in exchange for the mares and the Nash, and enough cash left over to put a down payment on another, slightly older car, which Barney happened to remember he had for sale. They had both won in the trade. Only Mrs. Feeney had lost.

Fergus went home in triumph, proud of his new team and anxious to show them off and brag about how he had beat Barney Gass in a horse trade. Whether he'd actually scammed Barney was immaterial. He'd edit the story enough so that there could be no question at all about his sagacity as a horse trader. Besides, Fergus was still bragging about the scam he'd pulled on the *Bangor Daily News*.

Fergus was an ardent saltwater fisherman, making several trips a year to fish for cod and haddock off Matinicus Island in outer Penobscot Bay. He had a lobsterman relative or two down around Stonington and went out with them for free, helping them pull their daily traps, then fishing for the rest of the day. One spring Fergus had hooked onto a large shark, which his relative shot and would have used for chum. But Fergus would hear none of that. He wanted to take his nearly eight-foot shark home.

After some haggling, it was agreed he could have the shark. They loaded it aboard his battered truck and he headed for Milford.

It was a late Friday afternoon when he got home. He strung up the shark, head down, from the limb of a large oak tree in his front yard, right by Sunkhaze Stream. It had been a wet spring, and the stream and river were still high. A perfect situation for a hoax.

After the shark was hung, Fergus posed beside it with an eighteen-foot bamboo fishing pole, of the kind used to catch pickerel, hornpout, perch, and bluegills. Word soon spread around the neighborhood about Fergus's fish, and people came to view it. Fergus swore that he had caught it early that morning while fishing for eels. And he was believed, particularly when he described the school of sharks he had seen swimming in the deeper water of the river, only yards away. Some even went home to get their own gear in hopes of catching a shark themselves.

Fergus was so successful in conning his neighbors that he decided to go for more. On Saturday morning he called the *Bangor Daily News* and told them about his remarkable catch. They took his story hook, line, and sinker, as the saying goes, and said they would send a reporter and cameraman right up. Fergus didn't make thirty-cent toll calls often, but this was going to be worth every cent.

In due course the reporter arrived with his cameraman in tow. He was a young cub, green and gullible, and he hung on every word of Fergus's tale of how he had nearly been pulled into the school of bloodthirsty sharks as he hung on doggedly to this one. He said he would certainly have been killed if Mrs. Feeney hadn't come to his rescue and shot the shark with his 30'06 Springfield hunting rifle and helped him drag in the carcass. Of course, he showed the reporter the bullet holes.

"Actually," he said, "I had to hitch up my hoss to pull the barstid up the bank. And we had to be careful, 'cause the head was still snappin'."

The news team took several pictures of Fergus with his eight-foot shark and departed. There he was on the front page on Monday morning, with a lengthy story about his miraculous catch and escape. There was comment that no shark had ever been spotted that far above tidewater before, and some wonderment that the sharks had navigated several dams. The story was a triumph that sustained him for a year or more. He even thought about having his shark stuffed, but by that time you needed to stand fifty feet upwind of the creature.

But after buying his new team of horses, Fergus was busy recounting his trials and successes with the new geldings. He was training them for field work and for showing and pulling. He had a theory about horses that he frequently extolled to other horse owners, whether farmer or woodsman. Simply put, it was that you could tell a strong and valuable horse by the amount of digestive gas it emitted while working. And in Fergus's words, he had, "Never seen a pair of hosses who farted as long and often as Hans and Fritz."

Of course his contention was disputed, and there were long discussions of its merit around the stove in the post office. According to Fergus, the theory went like this: "Yer want a good hoss. It needs to be healthy and to keep a hoss healthy, yer got to feed it well. If a hoss has lots of good feed and is healthy, it's goin' to digest its hay and oats real good. That means it will make lots of gas, which it's got to pass. If it don't pass gas, it'll bloat, and a bloated hoss is too uncomfortable to work good. So a fartin' hoss is sure to be a good hoss, and my team is the fartin'est pair of hosses I ever see."

It was a hard bit of logic to prove wrong. Fergus had the edge because his horses were healthy and they were beginning to win pulling contests, during which they publicly produced manure and gas. Any opponents to Fergus's theory had to prove that Fergus's evidence was, at best, unscientific and, at worst, probably immaterial. Meanwhile, Fergus basked in the notoriety of his now-famous farting horses.

He basked, that is, until the horses were about six years old and engaged in the summer haying season. Fergus cut twenty acres of his own hay each year. Hay prices were fairly stable in the '30s, and the demand was still good. After cutting his own hay, Fergus often cut hay on nearby farms that were no longer active as farms. The hay on these fields was often very cheap to buy standing, and sometimes free, if he kept the fields manured.

A mile or two from Sunkhaze Farm there was a small area known as the French settlement. Only one of its farms was still active, and that only as a dwelling place. The hayfields were up for grabs. And Fergus was the grabber. He hayed them and kept them "dressed" with ample applications of cow manure. And he produced an abundance of hay to sell. It was a great source of extra income, since Fergus paid no taxes on the land and spent no cash for additional fertilizer.

That summer the crop was extra bountiful, thanks to a cool and rainy spring. Fergus's horses seemed to love pulling the mower, stepping lively to the tune of the sicklebar as it whirred back and forth in the tall grass. Hans was the better for mowing, since he maintained a more steady pace. Fritz was the horse of choice for tedding and raking, but each could do either task, if necessary. The season was a huge success, and Fergus had thirty tons of prime fescue, timothy, and clover hay for sale in the winter, when the prices were higher.

The last few days of the season had proven very hot and dry. Hay could be made in a day because of the light winds, producing top-quality hay still showing green. Fergus enjoyed thinking about the winter's steady cash flow as he gleaned the last scatterings of the season. He took a break about once an hour to swill down some cold switchel to quench his thirst and to allow the horses a brief cooling off as they grazed on some green grass.

Finally, his hayrick was full. Had there been another forkful of hay, it wouldn't have stayed on the load. It was late afternoon, and Fergus was hot and sweaty. The switchel jug was nearly empty, but its tart mix of vinegar, molasses, and spring water was a great thirst quencher and he swigged down the last of it as the horses grazed on the hay stubble. Then Fergus loaded his pipe with Edgeworth Ready Rub tobacco, tamped it down good, and lit up for his first smoke since the nooning. The first puff was sweet and heady. It was time to go, and he would enjoy his pipe on the half-hour trip to the barn. Fergus gave the reins a slap on the horses' backs, shouting, "Let's go boys. C'mon, Fritz. C'mon Hans. Let's bring it in." Hans and Fritz reacted with alacrity, knowing the feedbag awaited them in the barn. They were off at almost a trot.

Things went well until they crossed the Maine Central tracks and approached the left turn onto Route 2. True to form, the horses were performing well, even though they were tired. The heavy load of hay caused them to strain in the harness, expelling gas as they did. Fergus was gleeful at the prospect of his haying rewards and a brief rest over the weekend. He sucked on his pipe, gave the reins a slap, and shouted, "Fart, you barstids, fart! You done a great job, and you'll get double oats tonight!"

The highway was clear except for a truck far to the right, coming slowly enough to allow the hayrick to enter the highway. Another slap of the reins, and they were headed south and home for sure. The team was in a real trot now, smelling the barn. Fergus was on his feet, urging them on, when the blare of a horn sounded and the truck that had seemed so far back and slow-moving went careening past them. The horses shied, lifted their tails, and both farted like they never had before. His teeth clenched on the pipestem, Fergus sucked on his pipe, causing the still nearly full bowl to glow hot and red just as the methane from the tremendous double fart went past his head. There was a whooshing thump, a flash of flame, and the sweet smell of burning hay. Disaster had struck.

The truck never slowed, passing the rearing horses as Fergus yanked and pulled on the reins to halt the team. His crew, riding on the back of the rick, were already off and grabbing at the bridles. They succeeded quickly, and Fergus jumped from the rick, yelling, "Unhitch the hosses! Unhitch the hosses!"

In seconds the horses were free, even though they continued to shy. As soon as the trace chains dropped, they bolted away from the hayrick, which was now blazing hotly. Fergus dug in his heels and heaved back on the reins to halt them. It was touch and go for a moment or two, but Fergus was very strong and a good teamster, and he pulled them to a stop.

Alas, there was no hope for the hayrick. It was a pyre, dead center in the middle of Route 2. Fergus, now completely bereft of his three-day stubble, most of his eyebrows, and all his lashes, hailed a passing motorist to hitch a ride for one of his crew, so that the fire department in Milford could be called.

The firetruck arrived a half-hour later to put out the flames on the still-burning rick. The hay had burned so quickly that the front wheels, wagon tongue, and wagon box were merely charred. The rear wheels were burned some, and the axle grease had run out of the hubs and burned on the ground. The hayrick itself was a total loss, but it was homebuilt of small oak and maple saplings, and it could be rebuilt easily enough.

What suffered the most damage was Fergus's ego. He didn't mind making others the focus of one of his pranks, but he wasn't a good loser. He knew he would be the butt of some heavy-handed humor in the coming months. News of his disaster would go with the firemen and spread like his hayrick fire. He imagined the coming jibes, "Ain't you shaving with a hayrick anymore, Fergus? Looks like you could use a good shave this mornin'. Get yerself all het up at the same time on a cold mornin' like this." But by the time he went after the mail at half past five, he was prepared to face the jeers at the store.

He strode in, all bravado and smiles, greeting the gang around the stove with, "Guess you fellas heerd about my hayrick fire. That's the damnedest thing ever could happen. I been tellin' yer right along them hosses of mine was just super-farters. Well, if yer didn't believe me before, yer gotta now. I jist never know how powerful they are. When they blasted me this afternoon, that gas was so heavy and dense that static electricity jist set it off." Fergus made no mention that he was foolishly smoking his pipe while seated in a load of hay. No use in providing fuel for a firestorm of sarcastic commentary on an already bad situation.

"'Course, there's some good come of the fire. I got me the closest shave I've had in years. Took them whiskers of mine right down to the quick, and all in a flash, too." There was no denying that statement, since Fergus's face was as clean and pink as a newborn's rump.

"But I'm jist happy they didn't backfire like a car does, or there'd be hossflesh clear to Costigan Village and I'd most likely be a charred corpse floatin' downriver by now. I learnt my lesson real good. From now on each of them hosses is going to have his own drag chain to drain off the static electricity. I ain't trustin' to their shoe calks no more. With hosses that are heavy farters, you can't be too careful, and that's a well-grounded fact."

20

THE TROUT

Back to the pool. I loved the pool. I always had good luck there, and the morning's bright sun and warmth presaged an especially good day. The stream made a sweeping arc around a huge boulder and became quite wide as it did so. The far bank, thirty feet away, was heavily aldered, the bushes growing outward over the water, which was deep and dark under them. The current swept down from my left, as I stood at the bank. It curled into the pool, eddying and swirling around the submerged bushes.

I trod lightly through the knee-high grass on my approach to the edge of the bank, lest my footsteps send vibrations into the pool. Trout spooked easily, I knew. They could feel the vibrations of my steps and might go deep in the pool, refusing to take any lure.

At the very apex of the bend where the stream curled to either side of me, I made my first cast, upstream. It was a good cast. The line swished over the water. The lure landedwith a plop in one of the swirling eddies about three feet from the alders on the far side. The current snatched up the line, sucking the lure down into obsidian depths under the bushes, where I could feel it being yanked and pulled about by the water.

There had to be trout there, ravenous and waiting in the depths for the current to bring them breakfast. I imagined a brookie, its rainbow spots dulled by the gloom, just waiting for my lure. My heartbeat quickened. I knew it was going to happen. I knew it.

Even so, the strike was vicious—and surprising. I had thought I was ready, sure in the knowledge that the trout was there, but the force of the strike still caught me off guard. For a few moments the trout raced with the lure while line snaked off the end of the rod. My reaction was almost too late, but I snapped the rod up, setting the hook, and the hook held. I had my trout on the line.

It was a big one. I'd never hooked onto anything that size before, and panic set in. I would lose it. I'dnever bring it to shore. My panic increased, because I wanted to land this trout more than I'd ever wanted to do anything in my life before.

I concentrated my thoughts on the rod. I fought down my panic by countering the efforts of the trout to free itself of the hook. I was unskillful at first, overplaying my moves—too much slack, then too tight—but I learned, and the hook continued to hold. My skill improved with every lunge of the trout that I successfully countered. I began to feel elated, and my confidence grew.

I could land the bugger. I would land the bugger. I became the master now, playing the trout with my rod and reel in a truly virtuoso performance. Twice the trout leapt high of the water, twisting its head and shaking the lure and hook. Each time I saw the size and beauty of the fish I felt the chill goose bumps of exhilaration. I had to land it.

The trout was tiring. As it weakened, I brought it across the pool, out of the shadows of the alders, into the bright sunlight. It was close to the surface now, swimming in short circular dashes, then resting, tired but still not taken.

Now to land it. I had no net and the water was nearly a foot below the bank. I had only the strength of the hook to get it on shore. I nearly panicked again as I saw that the hook was barely caught in the upper lip of my prize. It would never stay. I'd lose it as soon as it broke water, but I had to try. I had to do it. I had to land it.

My line was short now, only three feet to the trout. I gave the rod a strong flip. It bendt into a bow, the line tight and beaded with water droplets. I pulled upwards as I flipped the rod, and the trout surged from beneath the surface, arcing into the air over my head. It was free of the hook as it sailed gracefully into the tall grass ten feet behind me. It was a clean catch, a beautiful catch!

I threw down my rod and dashed for the trout. It flashed into view as it flopped about in the grass. I was on it. I had it in my hands, two fingers in the gill slits, and held it up in the morning sun. A beauty, a rainbow hued, dazzling beauty of a trout with a streak of orange along its flanks superimposed over the rainbow of spots. Not a record fish, but very respectable. Two pounds, maybe. Bigger than any trout I'd ever caught. Bigger than any Dad had ever caught.

My heart was hammering in my chest. My temples pounded. I wanted to hug the trout, to somehow share my joy in catching such a prize with the fish itself. I held it at arms length, seeing the gill covers expanding and contracting as they sought water.

And then I knew that I could share my joy in only one way. I had bested the fish, and this elateed me, but greater pleasure could be mine. I walked to the edge of the stream, placed the trout gently in the water, and released it. It stayed for a long minute, then with a mighty flip of its tail, disappeared into the deep hole of the pool.

I watched it go. My elation and pleasure were no longer a thing of the moment. They would always be there when I thought of my trout, the one I caught and kept in my heart.